On Location 2

Reading and Writing
for Success in the Content Areas

Thomas Bye

McGraw-Hill

On Location 2 Student Book, 1st Edition

Published by McGraw-Hill ESL/ELT, a business unit of The McGraw-Hill Companies, Inc., 1221 Avenue of the Americas, New York, NY 10020. Copyright © 2005 by the McGraw-Hill Companies, Inc. All rights reserved. No part of this publication may be reproduced or distributed in any form or by any means, or stored in a database or retrieval system, without the prior written consent of The McGraw-Hill Companies, Inc., including, but not limited to, in any network or other electronic storage or transmission, or broadcast for distance learning.

ISBN: 0-07-288677-3
1 2 3 4 5 6 7 8 9 QPD/QPD 11 10 09 08 07 06 05

ISBN: 0-07-111907-8 (International Student Book)
1 2 3 4 5 6 7 8 9 QPD/QPD 11 10 09 08 07 06 05

Editorial director: Tina B. Carver
Executive editor: Erik Gundersen
Senior developmental editor: Mari Vargo
Developmental editors: Fredrik Liljeblad, Stephen Handorf
Production manager: Juanita Thompson
Cover designer: Wee Design Group
Interior designer: Wee Design Group
Artists: Burgundy Beam, Randy Chewning, Greg Harris, Albert Lorenz, Judy Love, Anni Matsick, Yoshi Miyake, George Ulrich
Photo Researchers: David Averbach, Tobi Zausner
Skills Indexer: Susannah MacKay

INTERNATIONAL EDITION ISBN 0-07-111907-8
Copyright © 2005. Exclusive rights by The McGraw-Hill Companies, Inc., for manufacture and export. This book cannot be re-exported from the country to which it is sold by McGraw-Hill. The International Edition is not available in North America.

www.esl-elt.mcgraw-hill.com

The *McGraw·Hill* Companies

Acknowledgments

The authors and publisher would like to thank the following individuals who reviewed the *On Location* program at various stages of development and whose comments, reviews, and assistance were instrumental in helping us shape the project.

Carolyn Bohlman
Main East High School
Chicago, IL

Claire Bonskowski
Fairfax Public Schools
Fairfax, VA

Karen Caddoo
Sheridan Public Schools
Sheridan, CO

Florence Decker
El Paso MS/HS
Franklin, TX

Trudy Freer-Alvarez
Houston Independent School District
Houston, TX

Maryann Lyons
Francisco Middle School
San Francisco, CA

Susan Nordberg
Miami, FL

Jeanette Roy
Miami-Dade County Public Schools
Miami, FL

Steve Sloan
James Monroe High School
North Hills, CA

Leslie Eloise Somers
Miami-Dade County Public Schools
Miami, FL

Marie Stuart
San Gabriel Unified School District
San Gabriel, CA

Susan J. Watson
Horace Mann Middle School
San Francisco, CA

About the Author

Thomas Bye is an educator and consultant in second language learning and teaching. He was a high school teacher and has served as coordinator of bilingual education as well as director of curriculum and strategic planning for a large school district. He has written other programs for English Learners. He is an adjunct faculty member at St. Mary's College. He holds a Ph.D. in linguistics from UCLA.

Dedication

On Location is dedicated to my family, David Bohne and Chipper.

Scope and Sequence

Unit	Readings	Genres/ Writing Tasks	Reading Strategies	Word Work/ Spelling and Phonics
1 Can We Talk? page 2	Magazine interviews with Alex Rodriguez and Christina Vidal	Interviews	Skimming	Homophones Spelling the /ā/ sound as in *fame* and *play*
2 Animals Nobody Loves page 20	Selections from *Animals Nobody Loves* and *The Unhuggables*	Short informational reports	Taking notes Listing what you know	The suffixes -*y* and -*ing* Spelling the /ch/ sound as in *check* and *kitchen*
3 I Made It Myself! page 38	Instructions for making Halloween make-up and costumes	How-to instructions	Drawing a picture Predicting	Compound words Spelling the /ō/ sound as in *hole* and *boat*
4 Trying to Be Cool page 56	Selections from "Stupid Things I Did to Be Cool" from *Consumer Reports for Kids*	Personal narratives	Questioning the author Predicting	The suffix -*er* and -*or* in nouns Pronouncing words with the letters *gh*
5 Who Eats What? page 74	Selections about food chains from *Who Eats What?*	Explaining a process	Taking notes Making diagrams	Compound words that are animal names Spelling the /o͞o/ sound as in *food* and *blue*

Grammar	Organization	Style	Writing Conventions	Content Area Connections	Links to Literature
Wh- questions	Organizing information in an interview	Posing questions that get interesting answers	Sentence-level punctuation	Civics	Portrait poem
Subject-verb agreement with present tense verbs	Writing rich paragraphs: topic sentence and supporting sentences	Using adjectives to make writing vivid	Serial commas	Natural science	Poem "Acro-Bat," by Kenn Nesbitt
Imperatives	Organizing steps in a time sequence	Using specific words in how-to instructions	Symbols that stand for words	Consumer Economics Math	Poem "Best Mask," by Shel Silverstein
Simple past tense	Describing events in a time sequence	Writing for your audience: formal vs. informal language	Commas with *when*	Civics	Poem "Motto," by Langston Hughes
Present vs. past tense	Organizing parts of a process	Combining sentences with *that* clauses	Commas with examples	Science	Poem "Links in a Food Chain"

Scope and Sequence

Unit	Readings	Genres/ Writing Tasks	Reading Strategies	Word Work/ Spelling and Phonics
6 Real-Life Heroes page 92	True stories about rescues from *National Geographic World*	True stories	Predicting	Compound words derived from nouns and verbs plus their objects or prepositions Pronouncing words with the letters *oo*
7 Nature's Fury page 110	First- and third-person descriptions of natural disasters	Describing an event	Visualizing	Synonyms Pronouncing words with the letters *ou*
8 Drugs: The True Story page 128	Persuasive pamphlets against drugs and tobacco use	Persuasive writing	Identifying the main purpose Skimming	Prefixes that mean "not" Pronouncing words with the letters *ea*
9 I Love Jell-O®! page 146	"Reviews" of Jell-O® and oatmeal	Evaluations	Visualizing Summarizing	Antonyms Spelling the /j/ sound as in *jam* and *badge*
10 Let's Debate! page 164	Articles from *Junior Scholastic* that present debates	Debates	Identifying facts and opinions Skimming	Word families Spelling the /or/ sound as in *for* and *four*

Grammar	Organization	Style	Writing Conventions	Content Area Connections	Links to Literature
Adverbial time clauses	Organizing the action of a narrative	Writing titles and leads that grab the reader's attention	Exclamation points	Civics Health	Tall tale: "Paul Bunyan and the Gumberoos"
Review of the past tense	Describing an event	Using action-packed verbs Using similes	Sentence combining	Natural science	Myth: "The Turtle Tale"
Gerunds as subjects and objects	Organizing opinions, facts, and examples in persuasive writing	Using subheadings for clarity	Dashes	Health	Excerpts from *Go Ask Alice*, the diary of a teen drug user
Adverbial clauses of condition (*if* clauses)	Justifying an opinion with reasons, details, and facts	Using stand-out adjectives	Commas with sentence-starting adverbs	Consumer Economics Health	Review of Shel Sliverstein's *Falling Up* Poem "Tattooin' Ruth," by Shel Silverstein
Modals of persuasion	Organizing an argument	Using quoted speech to support an argument	Punctuation with quotes	Civics Health	Poem "How to Successfully Persuade Your Parents to Give You More Pocket Money," by Andrea Shavick

To the Student

Welcome to *On Location*! This book is written just for you. *On Location* will help you learn English while you explore the world.

You will read and write about our world—about the most feared animal in the sea and about people who survived earthquakes and tornadoes!

You will read and write about interesting people—other students just like you, a famous baseball star, and real-life heroes.

Should junk food be banned from school cafeterias? You will find out what other students think and express your own ideas in writing.

You will read works by famous poets and poems by students. Then you'll write your own poems.

You will learn new words and skills that will help you in your other classes, such as math, science, social studies, and geography.

Best of all, you will get to work with others—talking, thinking, and making things as you learn English together.

This is going to be a great year. Enjoy the learning process!

Tom Bye

To the Teacher

Welcome to *On Location*—a three-level reading and writing program that provides an enrichment approach to language and literacy development. Specially designed for middle and high school students at beginning to intermediate levels, *On Location* provides a gradual onramp to academic English, allowing English learners the time they need to develop powerful academic reading, writing, and communications skills.

The *On Location* program offers a research-based approach that honors the findings of the National Reading Panel regarding the direct teaching of reading skills combined with the promotion of instructional practices that develop language and literacy through a focus on comprehension. *On Location* also supports the principles of the Cognitive Academic Language Learning Approach (CALLA), teaching learning strategies that help students succeed across the curriculum.

The program recognizes that learning to read and write is developmental, requiring the acquisition of listening and speaking skills and high levels of student engagement. *On Location* provides students with the direct skills instruction they need to master state and local standards within the context of meaningful communication.

On Location promotes the reading-writing connection through a focus on key academic genres—the kinds of writing students encounter in content-area classes and on high-stakes tests. Students read selections that describe, tell a story, analyze, explain, justify a position, and persuade. And they explore the organizational and stylistic features of each genre as they produce their own writing.

PROVIDING AN ON-RAMP TO ACADEMIC LANGUAGE

Student Books

On Location is organized into three levels. Book 1 enables students to meet beginning-level standards for reading, writing, and oral language. Reading selections are fewer than 100 words in length, building basic fluency and comprehension skills. By the end of Book 1, students are able to read simple paragraphs and write well-formed, connected sentences.

Book 2 enables students to meet early intermediate standards. Reading selections are under 300 words in length, providing access to authentic text materials. By the end of Book 2, students are able to read simple multi-paragraph selections and write related paragraphs.

Book 3 enables students to meet intermediate-level standards. Reading selections are less than 800 words in length, providing an onramp to academic text. By the end of Book 3, students are able to produce simple essays—writing that informs, explains, analyzes, and persuades.

The *On Location* books are organized into ten engaging units, each focusing on a particular nonfiction reading and writing genre. Every reading is authentic—giving students opportunities to read a variety of real-world text selections. Because the reading selections come from sources such as *Junior Scholastic* and *Time for Kids*—as well as the Internet—they are always engaging and help students connect to the world around them.

In each unit, students have the opportunity to produce the type of writing that the unit's reading selection exemplifies. Incorporating a "backwards build-up" model, this is how a unit works—

- Students begin by connecting the topic of the unit's reading selections to their own lives and by developing key vocabulary they will need to read with understanding.
- Students tackle a word analysis skill and explore a grammatical structure they will encounter in each reading.

- As students read the selections that model the genre, they work at building fluency and develop reading strategies that help them become active readers.
- After reading, students explore the organization patterns and stylistic features of the selections.
- Students then produce their own writing as they move through the stages of the writing process that culminates with an oral presentation to classmates.

Along the way, students engage in structured listening and speaking activities that promote thinking and discussion, develop understanding, and build motivation. They explore sound/spelling relationships of words and learn common written conventions.

Each unit opens doors to academic content. Students explore topics in science, social studies, and geography and learn essential academic vocabulary and skills to help them tackle grade-level content across the curriculum. Students also read and respond to a literature selection in each unit that relates to the content of the readings in that unit.

On Location is designed for use in a variety of classroom settings.

SCENARIOS	TIME FRAME	STRATEGIES FOR USE
1: **On Location** serves as the primary instructional program.	12–18 hours/unit	Complete all Student Book and Practice Book activities. Implement all suggestions in the Teacher's Edition. Use all components of the On Location assessment system.
2: **On Location** supplements an adopted basal program, providing students with intensive reading/writing instruction.	8–12 hours/unit	Complete sections B through H in the Student Book. Complete selected Practice Book activities. Use Teacher's Edition suggestions as needed.
3: Selected units from **On Location** supplement an adopted basal program, providing opportunities to read and write non-fiction.	5–8 hours/unit	Complete sections B, C, F, G, and H in the Student Book. Use Teacher's Edition suggestions as needed.

Practice Books

Each level of On Location includes a corresponding **Practice Book**. The Practice Book provides students with the opportunity to master the reading skills, vocabulary, and grammar introduced in the Student Book while allowing them to evaluate their own writing and practice test-taking skills. Activities allow students to further explore unit topics, respond to literature selections, and discover how much they learned by completing the activities and writing tasks in the Student Books.

Audio Program

An **audio program** also accompanies each level of On Location. The audio program includes activities that develop social and academic listening skills in addition to recordings of all of the reading selections.

Phonics Book

On Location Phonics, which can be used as an introduction to *On Location* or in parallel fashion with Book 1, provides systematic, explicit instruction that helps students who are new to English hear the sound patterns of their new language and use knowledge of sound-letter relationships to read and write high-frequency words and phrases that they hear and see around them. Incorporating a "fast-track" approach, this optional component enables newcomers to learn both language and content from day one. Teaching notes at the bottom of each student page make *On Location Phonics* a self-contained program.

PROMOTING STAFF DEVELOPMENT

Wrap-Around Teacher's Editions

A wrap-around **Teacher's Edition** provides step by step guidance through every lesson, helping the teacher use best teaching practices to—

- introduce new vocabulary and important concepts through use of context
- use a three-stage process to develop active readers that involves reading aloud ("my turn"), having students share the reading task ("our turn"), and independent reading ("your turn")
- guide students through the stages of the writing process.

Teacher Training and Staff Development Video

The *On Location* program includes a powerful staff development video to support implementation of the program. The video provides strategies for teaching reading and writing from a language arts perspective—focusing on best practices such as pre-teaching vocabulary, use of read aloud/think aloud techniques, interactive reading, modeled writing, interactive writing, use of rubrics, and cooperative learning. The training video provides strategies for reading and writing in the content areas and demonstrates how *On Location* can be used effectively.

ENSURING ADEQUATE YEARLY PROGRESS

Assessment System

The *On Location* **Assessment System** includes a placement test, end-of-unit assessments, and end-of-level tests. Task-specific rubrics (or "ChecBrics") help students plan, revise, and evaluate their work.

Teachers can be sure that with its emphasis on academic reading and writing, *On Location* will help their school meet Adequate Yearly Progress (AYP) targets. The *On Location* assessment system supports district accountability efforts by providing tools that enable teachers to evaluate mastery of English language development/English language arts standards.

Welcome to On Location

On Location is a three-level supplementary series that teaches middle-school and high-school English learners to read and write non-fiction. Its gradual on-ramp approach gives learners the time and support they need to develop powerful academic reading, writing, and communication skills.

Tuning In activities provide **engaging listening passages** which introduce students to the topic of each unit.

Useful vocabulary is introduced throughout each unit. Students learn new words that will help them understand reading passages, discuss their ideas, and complete their own writing.

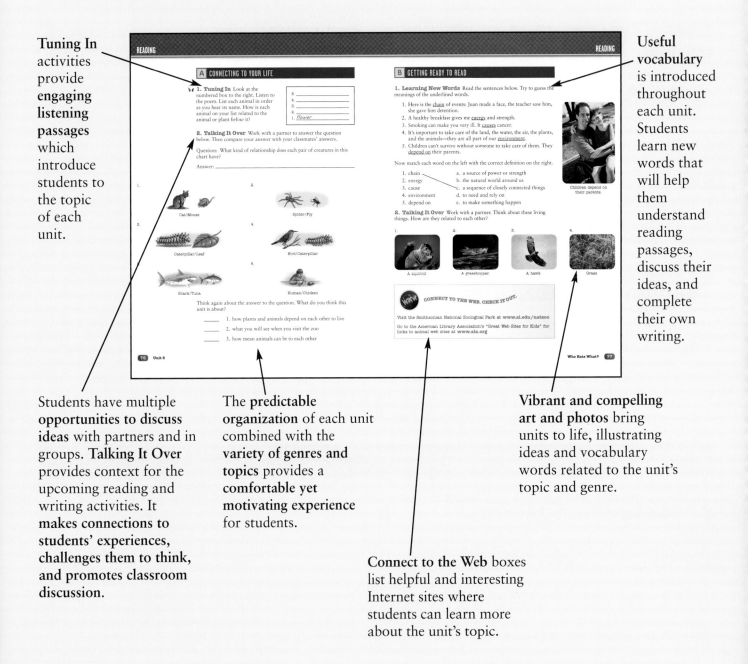

Students have multiple **opportunities to discuss ideas** with partners and in groups. **Talking It Over** provides context for the upcoming reading and writing activities. It **makes connections to students' experiences, challenges them to think, and promotes classroom discussion.**

The **predictable organization** of each unit combined with the **variety of genres and topics** provides a **comfortable yet motivating experience** for students.

Connect to the Web boxes list helpful and interesting Internet sites where students can learn more about the unit's topic.

Vibrant and compelling art and photos bring units to life, illustrating ideas and vocabulary words related to the unit's topic and genre.

Let's Read contains information about the upcoming reading selection and provides a question or a task that **helps students focus their reading.**

Before You Read activates background knowledge and connects students to the reading topic.

In **Unlocking Meaning,** three activities help students **understand what they are reading and encourage them to reread.** First, students identify the main idea, argument, or proposition. Second, they find details, reasons, or examples. And finally, they think more deeply about the reading.

Reading passages are accompanied by **relevant and practical reading strategies** that help students **develop a personal set of reading comprehension skills.**

Authentic non-fiction reading selections provide models for student writing while helping students build fluency and develop transferable comprehension skills and strategies for dealing with academic content.

Before You Move On is a post-reading activity that engages students in analysis and synthesis, retelling, summarizing, or acting on new information.

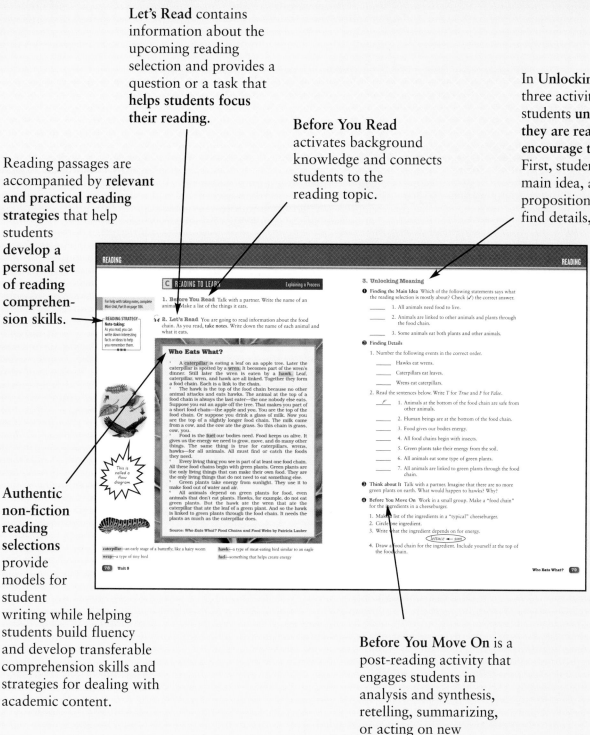

Grammar lessons provide instruction and practice around a grammar point that is relevant to the reading passages and the writing task in each unit.

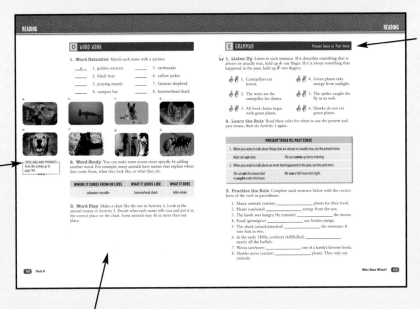

Spelling and Phonics activities help students develop knowledge of sound and spelling patterns in English.

Activities in the *Word Work* section develop word-analysis skills that help students figure out the meaning of vocabulary in the content areas.

Making Content Connections activities provide opportunities for students to complete tasks that relate to content areas, such as geography, science, and math.

A recording of every reading selection is included in the audio program.

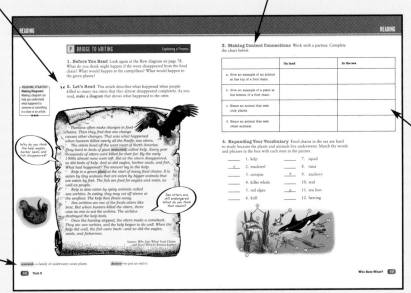

Graphic organizers and other tools promote higher order thinking skills, such as comparing, synthesizing, and inferencing.

New words are glossed below reading selections and are included in the glossary at the back of the book.

The sequence of activities in the *Writing Clinic* and the *Writer's Workshop* provides students with step-by-step procedures for producing a well-formed piece of academic writing. Students can use these procedures to complete writing assignments in their content area classes.

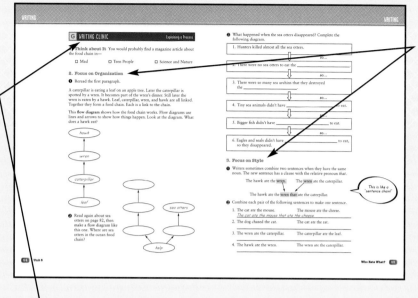

In **Focus on Organization** and **Focus on Style** activities, students **analyze the selection they have just read.**

In **Getting It Out** activities, students learn new strategies and work with lists, images, and graphic organizers to plan and develop their own writing.

Students work gradually toward completing their writing assignments. First, they spend time choosing the topic they'd like to write about.

After students have decided on their topics, they use a graphic organizer, a set of questions, or a specific set of instructions to guide them in their information gathering.

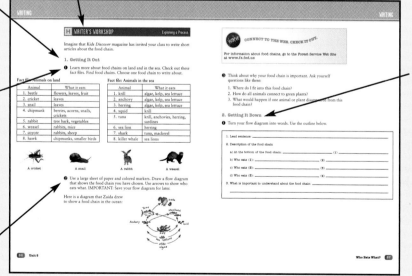

In **Getting It Down,** students turn their brainstorming and planning work into an outline and then a first-draft. Models are provided to demonstrate to students exactly what they are expected to do.

Mini-lessons in the *Writer's Workshop* focus on **writing conventions**, such as capitalization, punctuation, or spelling, that are relevant to the writing assignment.

In **Presenting It** activities, students share their work with their peers. They present their writing to their classmates, then give and receive constructive feedback.

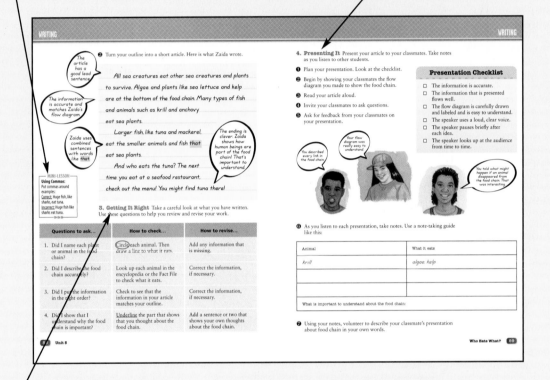

Getting It Right provides students with a combined checklist and rubric ("ChecBric") that helps them evaluate and revise their writing. The ChecBric, which is specific to each writing task, focuses on the skills that students have learned in the unit and provides a basis for evaluating level of performance on the task.

On Assignment activities provide fun exercises related to unit topics. Students learn more about each topic and interact with their classmates while they participate in class art shows, make posters, and conduct interviews.

In **Link to Literature** activities, students read poems or fiction selections and participate in guided discussions.

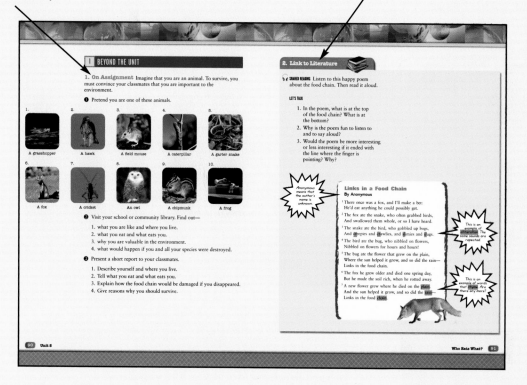

1 BEYOND THE UNIT

1. On Assignment Imagine that you are an animal. To survive, you must convince your classmates that you are important to the environment.

❶ Pretend you are one of these animals.

1. A grasshopper
2. A hawk
3. A field mouse
4. A caterpillar
5. A garter snake
6. A fox
7. A cricket
8. An owl
9. A chipmunk
10. A frog

❷ Visit your school or community library. Find out—

1. what you are like and where you live.
2. what you eat and what eats you.
3. why you are valuable in the environment.
4. what would happen if you and all your species were destroyed.

❸ Present a short report to your classmates.

1. Describe yourself and where you live.
2. Tell what you eat and what eats you.
3. Explain how the food chain would be damaged if you disappeared.
4. Give reasons why you should survive.

2. Link to Literature

SHARED READING Listen to this happy poem about the food chain. Then read it aloud.

LET'S TALK

1. In the poem, what is at the top of the food chain? What is at the bottom?
2. Why is the poem fun to listen to and to say aloud?
3. Would the poem be more interesting or less interesting if it ended with the line where the finger is pointing? Why?

Anonymous means that the author's name is unknown.

Links in a Food Chain
By Anonymous

1 There once was a fox, and I'll make a bet:
He'd eat anything he could possibly get.
2 The fox ate the snake, who often grabbed birds,
And swallowed them whole, or so I have heard.
3 The snake ate the bird, who gobbled up bugs,
And creepies and crawlies, and flimies and flugs.
4 The bird ate the bug, who nibbled on flowers,
Nibbled on flowers for hours and hours!
5 The bug ate the flower that grew on the plain,
Where the sun helped it grow, and so did the rain—
Links in the food chain.
6 The fox he grew older and died one spring day,
But he made the soil rich, when he rotted away.
7 A new flower grew where he died on the plain,
And the sun helped it grow, and so did the rain—
Links in the food chain.

This is an example of alliteration. The same sounds are repeated

This is an example of words that rhyme. Are there any more?

90 Unit 5

Who Eats What? 91

xvii

Can We Talk?

Read...

■ An interview with a famous baseball star.

■ An interview with a young TV actress.

Link to Literature

■ A portrait poem by a student.

Objectives:

Reading:
■ Reading magazine interviews with famous people
■ Strategy: Skimming
■ Literature: Responding to a poem

Writing:
■ Writing down an interview
■ Note-taking: Recording exact words

Vocabulary:
■ Recognizing homophones: Words that sound the same but have different meanings

Listening/Speaking:
■ Listening for facts
■ Asking information questions

Grammar:
■ Forming *Wh-* questions

Spelling and Phonics:
■ Spelling the /ā/ sound as in *fame* and *play*

Frankie Morales, star of the TV show *The Adventures of Max Jones*

BEFORE YOU BEGIN

Talk with your classmates.

1. Who is in the picture?
2. What can you guess about these two people?
3. Imagine that you are there. What question would you like to ask?

A CONNECTING TO YOUR LIFE

 1. Tuning In Listen to the interview with an actor. Write answers to the questions below.

a. Why is Frankie famous? _____

b. What is Frankie's favorite hobby? _____

c. In real life, is Frankie a good student? _____

d. What is Frankie's family like in real life? _____

2. Talking It Over Look at the pictures. Choose one person you would like to meet.

Write down a question you would ask him or her.

_____

Example question for Jennifer Lopez: _Where were you born?_

Jennifer Lopez, singer/actress

Tiger Woods, champion golfer

J. K. Rowling, writer (Harry Potter books)

Jaime Obregon, new kid in school

Read the title of this unit. What do you think you will learn to do in this unit? Check (✓) the correct answer.

_____ 1. how to write letters to friends

_____ 2. how to interview other people

_____ 3. how to describe other people

B GETTING READY TO READ

1. Learning New Words Read the sentences below. Try to guess the meanings of the underlined words.

1. Everybody knows Jennifer Lopez because she is an actress. Acting is her <u>claim to fame</u>.
2. My father told me I should work hard. That was good <u>advice</u>.
3. Tran got a job after school. He has an <u>opportunity</u> to make money.
4. Tina doesn't work for somebody else. She has her own <u>business</u>.
5. Dr. Vang is a medical doctor. Medicine is his <u>career</u>.
6. Rafael studies hard. He is <u>serious about</u> school.

Match each word or phrase on the left with the correct definition on the right.

1. claim to fame
2. advice
3. opportunity
4. business
5. career
6. be serious about

a. to care a lot about something
b. a chance to do something that will be good for you
c. the main reason a person is famous
d. a job you have trained for and will do a long time
e. an opinion about what to do or not do
f. buying and selling things

2. Talking It Over Work in a small group. Make a list of six famous people who have different careers. Write a sentence that describes each person's claim to fame. You can use the careers below or think of others.

EXAMPLE: *Jennifer Lopez is a movie actress*   .

a.

An athlete

b.

A writer

c.

An actor

d.

A world leader

e.

Someone who helps others

f.

A musician

C READING TO LEARN   Interviews

READING STRATEGY
Skimming:
When you skim, you read the whole passage quickly for general meaning. You don't read every word.

1. Before You Read Look at the photo. What do you know about this baseball player?

2. Let's Read Skim the interview below and answer this question: Who is Alex Rodriguez? Then read the interview carefully.

WHO: Alex Rodriguez

CLAIM TO FAME: *Star player for the New York Yankees. He is featured in* Backyard Baseball, *a video game.*

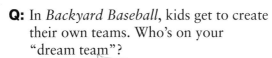

Q: In *Backyard Baseball*, kids get to create their own teams. Who's on your "dream team"?

A: I like some old-timers like Dale Murphy and Hank Aaron. My favorite all-time player is Cal Ripken Jr.

Q: What team did you root for when you were a kid?

A: I was born in New York, so I was a Mets fan.

Q: As a kid, were you the best player on the team?

A: No, because I always played with older kids.

Q: How should a kid handle a bad day on the field?

A: My number 1 advice is focus on academics. Keep working hard. Hard work will give you opportunities.

Q: Do you wish you had gone to college?

A: I made a promise to my mom to one day get a degree. I'd love to study business and own my own team.

Dale Murphy, Hank Aaron, and Cal Ripken Jr. are baseball stars from the past.

featured—having a part in (a movie or story)

old-timer—someone from the past

root for—to want someone (like a sports team) to win

fan—a person who likes something or someone a lot

handle—to deal with

degree—proof you have finished a course of study at a school—usually a university

own[1]—to have something because you bought it

own[2]—belonging to a person

3. Unlocking Meaning

❶ **Finding the Main Idea** Which sentence is true about Alex Rodriguez? Check (✔) the correct answer.

_____ 1. He is a professional baseball player.

_____ 2. He invents baseball video games.

_____ 3. He plays both baseball and basketball.

❷ **Finding Details** Choose the best ending for each sentence. Check (✔) the correct answer.

1. Alex's favorite baseball player of all time is—

_____ a. Hank Aaron.

_____ b. Cal Ripken Jr.

_____ c. Dale Murphy.

2. When Alex was a boy, he rooted for—

_____ a. the Texas Rangers.

_____ b. the San Francisco Giants.

_____ c. the New York Mets.

3. Alex advises young people—

_____ a. to play football instead of baseball.

_____ b. to play with older kids.

_____ c. to work hard in school.

4. In the future, Alex says he would like to—

_____ a. play for the Mets.

_____ b. make more video games.

_____ c. buy his own baseball team.

❸ **Think about It** Alex says he always played baseball with older kids. How do you think this helped him or hurt him? Talk with a partner.

❹ **Before You Move On** Write down one more question you would like to ask Alex.

Source: An interview with Alex Rodriguez, *TIME For Kids*, March 21, 2003. Used with permission from TIME For Kids Magazine.

D WORD WORK

1. Word Detective Many words sound the same but have different meanings. Complete each sentence. Read the sentences aloud.

1. The Yankees _____ the game.
   a. won
   b. one

2. I love my _____.
   a. ant
   b. aunt

3. Grandma can't _____ well.
   a. hear
   b. here

4. The dog has a long _____.
   a. tail
   b. tale

5. I want to _____ new clothes.
   a. by
   b. buy

6. I am _____ with my work.
   a. threw
   b. through

2. Word Study Learn more about words that sound the same but have different meanings.

Homophones are two words that have the same sound but different meanings. They can be spelled the same or differently.

EXAMPLES: Diego has a **son**.
Diego likes the **sun**.

Alex wants to **own** a baseball team.
Alex uses his **own** glove.

3. Word Play Work with a partner. Think of the homophone for each word below and write it down. Then make up sentences for *both* words and write them also. You can use a dictionary.

┌ **SPELLING AND PHONICS:** ┐
To do this activity, go to
page 192.
└ ■ ■ ■ ┘

1. four _____
2. eye _____
3. flour _____

4. be _____
5. two _____
6. no _____

7. lie _____
8. cent _____
9. our _____

E GRAMMAR   Information Questions

1. Listen Up Listen to each question. Point your thumb up 👍 if it sounds correct. Point your thumb down 👎 if it sounds wrong.

👍👎 1. What is your favorite sport?

👍👎 3. When did you come to the U.S.?

👍👎 2. Who your teacher is?

👍👎 4. Where you live?

2. Learn the Rule Information questions begin with question words like *what*, *when*, *who*, *where*, and *how*. Learn how to make information questions below, then do Activity 1 again.

INFORMATION QUESTIONS				
	Question word or phrase	Main verb *be* or helping verb	Subject	Main verb + rest of sentence
1. When the main verb is *be*, it goes before the subject.	*What* *Who*	*is* *are*	*your favorite food?* *his friends?*	
2. With all other verbs, use *do*, *does*, or *did* in the question.	*Where* *How* *When*	*does* *do* *did*	*he* *you* *Juan*	*live?* *like our school?* *come to the U.S.?*
3. The object of the verb in *how many* and *how much* questions is part of the question phrase.	*How many brothers*	*do*	*you*	*have?*

3. Practice the Rule Work with a partner. Read the answers. Then write the questions. Use question words or phrases.

1. Q: *What is your favorite sport* ? A: My favorite sport is soccer.
2. Q: _____ ? A: My best friend is Vladimir.
3. Q: _____ ? A: She lives in Los Angeles.
4. Q: _____ ? A: I came to the U.S. last year.
5. Q: _____ ? A: I have three sisters.
6. Q: _____ ? A: My favorite subject is math.

| F | **BRIDGE TO WRITING** | Interviews |

1. Before You Read Can you think of any kids who have their own TV shows? Make a list.

2. Let's Read Read the following interview with actress Christina Vidal. Once again, **skim** the questions then read the entire interview.

The Nickolodeon TV network makes shows for kids.

WHO: Christina Vidal, 19
CLAIM TO FAME: She plays Taina Morales on the Nickelodeon TV show *Taina*.

Q: *Is Taina a lot like you?*
A: Yes, in so many ways. We share the same dreams of wanting to become a star. We're both Puerto Rican. She goes to a performing-arts high school. Growing up in New York, I traveled an hour every day to the LaGuardia High School of Performing Arts.

Q: *What's it like being one of the first Latinas to star in their own show on U.S. TV?*
A: It feels great to be a part of something that shows Latinos in a different kind of light. I'm really proud to be a Puerto Rican. I want to show people that there don't need to be any stereotypes.

Q: *You also sing on the show. How serious are you about music?*
A: I love music and acting. I want to pursue both careers. Eventually, I'd like to record an album.

Source: An interview with Christina Vidal, *TIME For Kids,* March 9, 2001. Used with permission from TIME For Kids Magazine.

dreams—hopes for the future

performing arts—music, dance, or drama

in a different kind of light—in a different way

stereotype—an idea about a person based only on their race, religion, ethnic group, etc.

acting—playing someone in a movie or show

pursue—to do or try something

eventually—one day

3. Making Content Connections You have read interviews with two famous people. Who are the "stars" in your own class? Find out.

Do you write poetry?

Yes.

"Star" Search

Find someone who...	Name
1. writes poetry.	_____
2. is good at more than one sport.	_____
3. draws or paints.	_____
4. can play more than one instrument.	_____
5. has a good singing voice.	_____
6. comes from a really large family.	_____
7. likes to help other people.	_____
8. has a "superstar" personality.	_____

4. Expanding Your Vocabulary Imagine that you are interviewing someone. Read each situation and check (✓) the correct statement or question.

1. You begin the interview.
   - _____ a. "Let me tell you what I think."
   - _____ b. "Thank you for agreeing to talk with me."
   - _____ c. "Please give me another example."

2. You want to let the person know you are interested.
   - _____ a. "I don't have any more questions."
   - _____ b. "How boring!"
   - _____ c. "Tell me more!"

3. You want to let the person know you don't understand what they said.
   - _____ a. "I disagree with you."
   - _____ b. "I'm sorry. I didn't get that."
   - _____ c. "I'm not sure that's right."

4. It's time to end the interview.
   - _____ a. "Thank you for your time."
   - _____ b. "Could you begin by telling me about yourself?"
   - _____ c. "Can I ask you a few more questions?"

G WRITING CLINIC

1. Think about It What kinds of people usually give interviews to reporters? Check (✓) the correct answers.

_____ politicians

_____ parents

_____ TV stars

_____ teenagers

_____ athletes

_____ teachers

2. Focus on Organization

❶ An interview usually has a **heading**. The heading tells the reader who the person being interviewed is and why that person is interesting. Read the heading below.

> **WHO:** Alex Rodriguez
>
> **CLAIM TO FAME:** *Star player for the New York Yankees. He is featured in* Backyard Baseball, *a video game.*

❷ The **body** of the interview has questions and answers. Match each of the following questions with the correct answer.

1. Where were you born?
2. When did you begin playing baseball?
3. Who is your favorite baseball player?
4. What's the best part about being a baseball player?
5. What's the hardest part about being a baseball player?
6. What other sports do you like?

a. My all-time favorite is Cal Ripken Jr.
b. Golf and tennis.
c. In New York City.
d. I love the fans.
e. I have to travel a lot. I hate to be away from home.
f. When I was a boy.

❸ Interview questions often ask about personal information, the reason the person is famous, and the person's likes and dislikes. Work with a partner. Imagine you could interview either Alex Rodriguez or Christina Vidal. What would you ask? Complete the following chart.

Personal Information	Their claim to fame	Their likes and dislikes
Where do you live?	When did you start acting?	Do you like movies?

3. Focus on Style

❶ Good interview questions make the person say more than just "yes" or "no." Which of the following questions is better? Why?

Do you enjoy sports?

What sports do you enjoy most?

❷ Rewrite each of the following questions to make information questions. Begin your questions with words like these:

What...? What kind...? Who...? When...?
Where...? How...? How well...?

1. Do you like school? _What do you like about school?_

2. Are you good at sports? _____

3. Do you have lots of friends? _____

4. Do you do your homework every night? _____

5. Do you like TV? _____

6. Do you like music? _____

7. Are your classes easy or hard? _____

8. Have you lived in the U.S. long? _____

9. Do you like living in the U.S.? _____

H WRITER'S WORKSHOP   Interviews

For help with taking notes, complete Mini-Unit, Part A on page 182.

Imagine that you are a reporter for your school newspaper. You want to interview a person you know with a "claim to fame," perhaps a classmate or a family member.

1. Getting It Out

❶ Choose a person to interview. Ask yourself: What is this person's claim to fame?

on the honor roll

good at drawing

speaks four languages

❷ Think about good questions to ask. Make a chart. Use question words that will encourage the person to talk.

Personal information	Their claim to fame	Likes and dislikes
Where were you born?	How does it feel to...?	Which sport do you like best?
When did you come to the U.S.?	What is the best part about...?	Who is your favorite singer?

❸ Make a form like this one for taking interview notes. Write as many questions as necessary. Leave room after each question for the answers.

Name: _____

Reason I am interviewing this person: _____

Personal information: _____

Question #1: _____?

Answer: _____

❹ Interview the person.

1. Find out about the person's background.

2. Ask questions about the person's claim to fame.

3. Ask other questions to learn more about the person.

4. Write down the person's exact words.

5. Thank the person for talking with you.

2. Getting It Down

❶ Draft your interview.

1. Write the person's name at the top of a piece of paper. Write his or her claim to fame under the name.

> *WHO: William Vang*
>
> *CLAIM TO FAME: Speaks four languages*

2. Carefully copy each question and answer from your note-taking sheet. Put **Q:** in front of each question and **A:** in front of each answer. Use complete sentences.

> *Q: When did you come to the U.S.? How old were you?*
>
> *A: I came here when I was 40.*

3. Show the person the interview. Correct any mistakes.

I came here when I was 14... not 40!

❷ Read part of Juan's interview with William.

Juan puts a heading at the beginning of the interview.

Juan asks good questions.

WHO: William Vang
CLAIM TO FAME: Speaks four languages

Q: When did you come to the U.S.? How old were you?
A: I came here when I was 14.

Q: How many languages do you speak?
A: Four! I speak Hmong, Mien, French, and English.

Q: Which language you speak best?
A: I speak Hmong best! That's my native language.

Q: How did you learn to speak four languages so well?
A: I had good teachers—my family!

Juan writes William's exact words.

Oops! The helping verb "do" is missing in one of the questions!

3. Getting It Right Take a careful look at your interview. Use this guide to revise what you have written.

Ask yourself . . .	How to check . . .	How to revise. . .
1. Does my interview have a heading?	<u>Underline</u> the person's name and claim to fame.	Add the reason that you interviewed the person (claim to fame).
2. Did I ask good questions?	Did the person answer more than "yes" and "no"?	Ask the person follow-up questions that begin with words like *what*, *why*, *who*, *when*, and *how*.
3. Did I write each question correctly?	Ask a neighbor to check your questions.	Correct the word order in the question. Add a helping verb if you need to.
4. Did I record the person's exact words?	Ask the person you interviewed to read his or her answers.	Make any changes.

4. Presenting It Share your interview with others.

❶ Act out your interview with the person you talked to. If you interviewed someone from outside of class, ask a classmate to help you act out the interview.

❷ Ask for feedback on the interview.

1. On Assignment Your class will interview an adult at your school or from the community.

❶ Decide who you will interview.

Your principal	Another teacher	A police officer

❷ Invite the person to visit your class. Choose a date for the interview.

> Dear Ms. Ponce:
>
> Our class is interviewing interesting people. We would like to interview you. Would you have time to visit our class sometime soon?

> When did you become the principal of our school?
>
> Were you a teacher before?
>
> What did you teach?

❸ Make a list of interesting questions to ask.

❹ Choose one of your classmates to be the interviewer. Conduct the interview.

❺ Take notes as you listen. Write down the person's exact words.

❻ Ask follow-up questions.

What's the hardest thing about being a principal?

> Dear Ms. Ponce:
>
> Thank you for visiting our class yesterday. We enjoyed interviewing you. You are a very interesting person!
>
> Again, thank you for your time.
>
> Sincerely, Period 3 class

❼ Write a class "thank you" note to the person.

2. Link to Literature

🎧 **SHARED READING** A portrait poem reveals things about a person—just like an interview. Read this portrait poem written by a student. To make her poem fun to read, she tells some things about herself that are true and some things that are false!

LET'S TALK Answer the questions.

1. Which statements about Paula are probably true? Why?

2. Which statements are probably false? Why?

3. What can you say about Paula from her portrait?

JUST FOR FUN Write your own portrait poem. It should be ten lines long.

- Begin and end with "I am …"
- Write four truthful statements about yourself
- Write four "lies" about yourself. Make each one believable.

I am Paula Jones.

I am sixteen years old.
I ride wild stallions.
I collect foreign coins.
My sister has six fingers
on her left hand.
My mother and I always
get along.
Time has stood still for me.
My father is a spy in the CIA.

I am Paula Jones.

stallion—a male horse
CIA—Central Intelligence Agency

Animals Nobody Loves

Read...

- A short selection about a disgusting creature: the cockroach.

- A short selection about a scary animal of the sea: the shark.

Link to Literature

- "Acro-Bat," a poem by Kenn Nesbitt.

Objectives:

Reading:
- Reading an informational selection about nature
- Strategies: Taking notes, listing what you know
- Literature: Responding to a poem

Writing:
- Organizing an informational paragraph
- Writing a topic sentence and details
- Using adjectives to make writing vivid
- Making a class book

Vocabulary:
- Turning nouns and verbs into adjectives
- Learning names of types of animals

Listening/Speaking:
- Listening to descriptions
- Ranking
- Comparing animals

Grammar:
- Understanding subject-verb agreement

Spelling and Phonics:
- Spelling the /ch/ sound as in *check* and *kitchen*

A great white shark

BEFORE YOU BEGIN

Talk with your classmates.

1. Look at the picture. What do you see? How does the picture make you feel?
2. Read the caption. What type of shark is it?
3. What do you know about sharks? Help your teacher make a list.

A CONNECTING TO YOUR LIFE

1. Tuning In Listen to the description on the tape or CD. Look at the pictures below. Which one of these animals is the speaker talking about?

2. Talking It Over Work with a partner. Look at these animals. One of them does **not** belong with the others. Which animal is it? How do you know?

The five other animals share one thing: People do not like them! Talk about one reason that people don't like each animal. Share your reasons with your classmates.

EXAMPLE: *People don't like rattlesnakes because they can bite you.*

A spider

A dog

A rattlesnake

A cockroach

A crocodile

A rat

Read the title of this unit. What do you think this unit is probably about? Check (✓) the correct answer.

_____ 1. cute animals

_____ 2. pets

_____ 3. scary animals

B GETTING READY TO READ

1. Learning New Words Read the sentences below. Try to guess the meanings of the underlined words.

Dogs are loving creatures.

1. Rats eat garbage. Ugh! They are <u>disgusting</u>!
2. Crocodiles can crush other animals to death with their <u>powerful</u> jaws.
3. Rattlesnakes are <u>dangerous</u>. You can die from a rattlesnake bite!
4. A shark usually eats other fish, but if it is really hungry, it may <u>attack</u> and kill people.
5. Cockroaches can live in very hot places and very cold places. They can <u>survive</u> almost anywhere.
6. Dogs are very loving <u>creatures</u>. They usually don't bite.
7. The baseball game was <u>amazing</u>! It lasted for 18 innings.

Now, match each word on the left with the correct definition on the right.

1. disgusting   a. an animal
2. powerful   b. to try to hurt
3. dangerous   c. able to hurt or kill
4. attack   d. to stay alive
5. survive   e. very unpleasant and sickening
6. creature   f. very surprising and difficult to believe
7. amazing   g. very strong

2. Talking It Over Work in groups of three or four. Look at the animals on page 22. Rank them on the scale below. Use the new words you just learned to discuss your choices.

Most dangerous

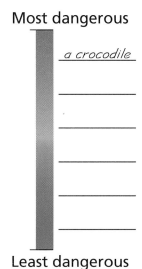

a crocodile

_____

_____

_____

_____

_____

Least dangerous

C READING TO LEARN — Short Informational Reports

1. Before You Read Most people really dislike cockroaches. What do you know about cockroaches? Why do people think cockroaches are so *disgusting*? Talk with a partner.

2. Let's Read Read this short report of information. The selection gives interesting and important information about cockroaches. As you read, **take notes** about things that make cockroaches so amazing.

Cockroaches

One foot equals 30.5 centimeters.

Cockroaches are really yucky. They look disgusting, they crawl all over the food left out in kitchens and people have a very hard time getting rid of them. But, like them or not, cockroaches are truly amazing creatures.

Few animals are better equipped for life on earth than they are. They can live almost anywhere, eat almost anything, and survive for weeks on almost nothing. They can withstand heat waves and cold spells.

When cockroaches scatter, they scurry away on long, strong legs at nearly one foot per second. At the same time they flatten themselves as thin as a dime and squeeze safely through cracks and crevices. Cockroaches are so successful at staying alive that they have survived for more than 350 million years—since before the age of dinosaurs.

Source: *The Unhuggables* by Victor Waldrup, Debbie Anker, and Elizabeth Blizzard

equipped for—made for

withstand—to experience something bad without damage

scatter—to run in different directions

scurry—to move fast

crevice—a narrow opening

dinosaur—a reptile that lived millions of years ago

3. Unlocking Meaning

❶ Finding the Main Idea Which of the following sentences talks about the most important idea from the article? Check (✔) the correct answer.

_____ 1. Cockroaches are stronger than humans.

_____ 2. Cockroaches are amazing.

_____ 3. Cockroaches are very hard to get rid of.

❷ Finding Details Read the second and third paragraphs of the article again. Then read the sentences below. Write _T_ for _True_ and _F_ for _False_.

___T___ 1. Cockroaches eat almost anything.

_____ 2. Cockroaches need to eat every day or they will die.

_____ 3. Cockroaches can live almost anywhere.

_____ 4. Cockroaches can't live in cold weather.

_____ 5. Cockroaches are easy to kill because they move slowly.

_____ 6. Cockroaches can move around in very tiny places.

_____ 7. Cockroaches were on Earth before dinosaurs.

❸ Think about It Cockroaches were on the Earth over 100 million years before dinosaurs! Dinosaurs disappeared 65 million years ago but cockroaches are still here today. Why do you think that cockroaches survived so long? Talk with a partner. Write three reasons.

350 million years ago   4,500 years ago

❹ Before You Move On The title of the article you just read is "Cockroaches." Read the article one more time. Can you think of a _more interesting_ title for the article? Write the title, then share it with your classmates.

New Title: _____

D WORD WORK

1. Word Detective Sometimes you can guess what a word means by looking for a smaller word or part of a word inside the longer one. The underlined words below are adjectives. Find the smaller words or parts inside the adjectives and write them down.

An adjective describes a person, place, or thing.

1. <u>dirty</u> animal
   smaller word: ___*dirt*___

2. <u>amazing</u> creature
   smaller word: _____

3. <u>scary</u> spider
   smaller word: _____

4. <u>disgusting</u> place
   smaller word: _____

2. Word Study You can make many nouns and verbs into adjectives by adding a short ending called a suffix. Look at the words below. Circle the suffix in each adjective. *Note:* sometimes the spelling changes a little when a noun or verb is changed into an adjective.

Drop the final -e when you add the ending -y or -ing.

-y			-ing		
sugar	→	sugary	surprise	→	surprising
freak	→	freaky	annoy	→	annoying

3. Word Play Work with a partner. Write an adjective for each word below by adding *–y* or *–ing*. Then choose five of the adjectives and write one sentence for each. *Note:* Some words can take either *–y* or *–ing*, but they will have different meanings. Use a dictionary.

Usually, you add -y to nouns and -ing to verbs to make adjectives.

1. ice
   *icy*_____

2. wind
   _____

3. interest
   _____

4. scare
   _____

5. creep
   _____

6. dirt
   _____

7. bore
   _____

8. excite
   _____

9. salt
   _____

10. sleep
    _____

11. confuse
    _____

12. blood
    _____

SPELLING AND PHONICS: To do this activity, go to page 192.

Sentences:

1. _____

2. _____

3. _____

4. _____

5. _____

E GRAMMAR   Subject-Verb Agreement

1. Listen Up Listen to each sentence. Point your thumb up 👍 if it sounds correct. Point your thumb down 👎 if it sounds wrong.

👍 👎 1. Cockroaches is really yucky.

👍 👎 2. Cockroaches are amazing creatures.

👍 👎 3. Cockroaches lives almost everywhere.

👍 👎 4. A cockroach run very fast.

2. Learn the Rule Learn how to make present tense verbs agree with their subjects. After you have learned the rules, do Activity 1 again.

SUBJECT-VERB AGREEMENT WITH PRESENT TENSE VERBS
1. When the subject is a singular noun or the singular pronoun *he, she,* or *it,* the verb ends in *–s* or *–es.*
*A cockroach **eats** almost anything.*
2. When the subject is a plural noun or the pronoun *I, you, we,* or *they,* the verb doesn't end in *–s* or *–es.*
*Cockroaches **like** to live in the dark.*
3. With the verb *be,* use *is* when the subject is a singular noun or the singular pronoun *he, she,* or *it.* Use *are* when the subject is a plural noun or the pronoun *you, we,* or *they.* Use *am* when the subject is *I.*
*A cockroach **is** a yucky insect.   Cockroaches **are** yucky insects.   I **am** afraid of cockroaches.*

3. Practice the Rule Read each sentence aloud. Circle the correct form of each verb.

1. Many people think spiders (is/are) scary creatures.
2. Many people (is/are) afraid of spiders.
3. Spiders (trap/traps) other insects in webs.
4. The black widow spider (is/are) very dangerous.
5. Rats (live/lives) everywhere.
6. Rats (spread/spreads) dirt and disease.

F BRIDGE TO WRITING   Short Informational Reports

1. Before You Read Work with a partner. Many people are afraid of sharks. What do you already know about sharks? **List** three things.

🎧 **2. Let's Read** Read about sharks. As you read, add one fact that you didn't know to your list.

> *Can you guess what a hammerhead shark looks like? What about a tiger shark?*

SHARK

The shark is the most feared animal in the sea. Some sharks are large and dangerous. Others are just a few feet long and eat small fish. Sharks come in many different sizes, shapes, and colors. Hammerheads, tiger sharks, and mako sharks have powerful jaws and razor-sharp teeth. Some sharks can bite three hundred times harder than a human.

The most dangerous shark is the great white shark. It usually swims in the open sea. But sometimes a great white shark may attack and kill swimmers with no warning. It may even attack small boats. Its large, saw-edged teeth can rip through wood and even metal. The great white shark has a huge appetite and will eat any animal or person that it finds in its path.

A great white shark

Source: *Animals Nobody Loves* by Seymour Simon

feared—frightening to people

warning—a sign of danger

metal—a material like steel, tin, or iron

appetite—hunger

path—way

3. Making Content Connections You have read about two animals that nobody loves: cockroaches and sharks. Now, work with a partner. Complete the chart below.

	Cockroach	Shark
1. What does it look like?	*six long legs, can be flat as a dime*	
2. Where does it live?		
3. What does it do?		

4. Expanding Your Vocabulary In the chart below, find the word in each row that *does not* go with the word in capital letters. Cross it out.

An insect

A fish

A reptile

A mammal

A bird

1. INSECT	mosquito	cockroach	~~crocodile~~
2. FISH	shark	eagle	piranha
3. REPTILE	crocodile	tiger	rattlesnake
4. MAMMAL	human	mosquito	lion
5. BIRD	eagle	Superman	parrot

A mosquito

A piranha

A tiger

An eagle

A lion

A parrot

G WRITING CLINIC   Short Informational Reports

1. Think about It In both readings in this unit, what is the author's purpose? Check (✓) the correct answer.

_____to scare you   _____to inform you   _____to persuade you

2. Focus on Organization

❶ Read the first paragraph again from one of the articles again. What is the paragraph about? Talk with a partner.

> The shark is the most feared animal in the sea. Some sharks are large and dangerous. Others are just a few feet long and eat small fish. Sharks come in many different sizes, shapes, and colors. Hammerheads, tiger sharks, and mako sharks have powerful jaws and razor-sharp teeth. Some sharks can bite three hundred times harder than a human.

The sentence in green tells us what the paragraph is about. It's called the topic sentence. A good paragraph has a topic sentence.

❷ Make an outline. Fold a piece of paper in half from top to bottom, then fold it again, creating four parts. Copy the topic sentence from the first paragraph in the top part. Next copy three important detail sentences from the paragraph.

(Topic sentence) *The shark is the most feared animal in the sea.*
(Detail #1)
(Detail #2)
(Detail #3)

❸ Now read the second paragraph from the sharks article again.

> The most dangerous shark is the great white shark. It usually swims in the open sea. But sometimes a great white shark may attack and kill swimmers with no warning. It may even attack small boats. Its large, saw-edged teeth can rip through wood and even metal. The great white shark has a huge appetite and will eat any animal or person that it finds in its path.

❹ Turn your paper over and use the other side to outline the second paragraph. This time, don't copy. Use your own words.

(Topic sentence)	
(Detail #1)	
(Detail #2)	
(Detail #3)	

3. Focus on Style

❶ This is a sentence that a student wrote about great white sharks. The sentence is interesting to read because it has two adjectives. Circle the adjectives.
They are large, dangerous animals.

❷ Work with a partner. Think of at least five animals that people do not like. Write the name of each animal in the correct place in the chart below.

	huge	large	small	tiny
dangerous	great white shark			
powerful				
disgusting				
scary				
annoying				mosquito

❸ Write a sentence about each animal. Use two adjectives in each sentence. Share your sentences with your classmates.

H WRITER'S WORKSHOP   Short Informational Reports

Write a book with your class called, "Creatures that Kids Love to Hate." Make a page for the book. Follow the directions below.

1. Getting It Out

❶ Begin by choosing an animal to write about. Look at the pictures below for ideas or choose another unlovable creature.

1. Spider

Important facts:

Usually harmless

Has eight legs

Spins a web to trap insects

Kills by biting and injecting poison

Usually bites people only when bothered

2. Rat

Important facts:

Small, furry mammal

Has very sharp teeth

Lives nearly everywhere in the world

Lives in garbage dumps

Lives in people's houses

Eats food that is left out

Carries fleas and can spread disease

3. Piranha

Important facts:

The most dangerous fish in the world

Has killed more humans than sharks

Is less than one foot long

Lives in rivers and streams in South America

Has razor-sharp teeth

Can eat the meat off a large animal
   or human in just a few minutes.

4. Skunk

Important facts:

Small mammal

Is usually peaceful

Eats insects and berries

Usually goes out only at night

Has white stripes along its back

Raises its tail to scare its enemies

Will spray bad-smelling liquid if
   bothered

❷ Print the name of your animal in capital letters at the top of a piece of paper. Fold the paper in one direction, then in the other, to make four sections. Number each section.

Write each of the following questions in one section. Then write words and ideas in each section that answer these questions:

1. What is it?
2. Where does it live?
3. What is it like?
4. Why do so many people dislike or fear it?

RAT	

1. What is it?
    a rodent
	2. Where does it live?
	    under houses
	    in attics
	    in garbage dumps
	    everywhere!

3. What is it like?
    small, furry animal
    has a long tail
    makes squeaky sounds
    runs or scurries very fast
    has sharp teeth ... can chew
        through wood and metal
    eats our food
    eats garbage
	4. Why do so many people dislike or fear it?
	    carries fleas that spread disease
	    sometimes bites people
	    gives me bad dreams!!!

 CONNECT TO THE WEB. CHECK IT OUT:

www.nationalgeographic.com/kids This site will help you learn more about creatures in nature. You will connect to National Geographic for Kids Magazine, which includes many articles about animals.

www.nwf.org/kids Web site for the National Wildlife Federation for Kids.

---MINI-LESSON---

Using Commas:
Put commas between words and phrases in a series:
They live under houses, in attics, and in garbage dumps.

2. Getting It Down

❶ Turn your notes into an outline. Take out another piece of paper. Fold your paper from top to bottom like you did before to make four parts. Write your topic sentence in the top part. Write one important detail in each of the three other parts. Use complete sentences.

(Topic sentence)

- -

(Detail #1)

- -

(Detail #2)

- -

(Detail #3)

---

❷ Now turn your paper over and make your outline into a paragraph. Begin your paragraph with your topic sentence. Here is what Juan wrote:

Has a good topic sentence.

Each detail about rats connects with the topic sentence.

> Many people fear and hate rats. These furry little rodents live nearly everywhere—under houses, in attics, and in garbage dumps. They love to eat smelly, rotting garbage. Rats carries fleas that spread disease.

Oops! The verb doesn't agree with the subject!

Adjectives make Juan's paragraph interesting to read.

3 Getting It Right Now take a careful look at what you have written. Use this guide to revise your paragraph.

Ask yourself...	How to check...	How to revise...
1. Does my paragraph have a good topic sentence?	<u>Underline</u> your topic sentence.	Add a sentence that tells what your paragraph is about.
2. Do the details relate to the topic sentence?	Put a check mark (✔) in front of each sentence that gives an example or detail.	Add sentences that give examples or details.
3. Do I use adjectives to make my paragraph interesting?	⟨Circle⟩ each adjective.	Add adjectives.
4. Does each verb agree with its subject?	Look at the chart on page 27. Does each verb follow the rules?	Correct each verb.

4. Presenting It Draw a picture of your animal—or clip a photograph from a magazine—to go with your paragraph. Share your work with your classmates.

❶ Begin by showing the picture of your animal and naming it.

❷ Read your paragraph aloud. Read slowly and speak clearly.

❸ Ask if anyone has any questions.

❹ Ask for feedback from your classmates.

1. On Assignment Bind all the student pages together to make a book. Have a two- or three-person production team make the book.

❶ Fold four or more 11″×17″ sheets of paper in half. Use a large needle to poke five holes through all the folded sheets so that they line up.

❷ Cut a 30-inch-long (one-meter) piece of thread. Thread your needle. Push the needle down through hole 1. Pull the thread through, but leave a four-inch (12-centimeter) tail so you can tie a knot later. Then go up through hole 2, down through hole 3, up through hole 4, down through hole 5, and back in the other direction. Tie and knot thread.

❸ Make the book cover. Cut two pieces of colored poster board a bit larger than the pages on all sides. Cut a strip of wide sticky tape about 16″ long. Place boards about $\frac{1}{4}$″ apart onto the sticky tape, then fold back each end of the tape to make the spine of the book sturdy.

❹ Set pages into the spine. Glue the first page onto one cover, then the last page onto the other cover.

❺ Carefully paste each picture and paragraph onto its own page. Number each page.

❻ Make a front cover for the book, showing the title, authors, and illustrators.

2. Link to Literature

SHARED READING Many people are afraid of bats. A bat looks like a mouse with wings. Read "Acro-Bat," a funny poem about a bat.

LET'S TALK Answer the following questions.

1. Why is the bat *exceptional*, or special?

2. What do we learn about bats in the poem? In real life, where do bats sleep?

3. Why is the poem funny?

Acro-Bat
by Kenn Nesbitt

My bat is a rather
exceptional bat.
You won't find him
sleeping in trees.
You see, he's a daredevil
acrobat—
He sleeps on a flying
trapeze.

Source: poetry4kids.com

Have you ever been to the circus? Have you ever watched a trapeze artist or a tightrope walker? Both are acrobats.

exceptional—very special

daredevil—someone who isn't afraid to do dangerous things

I Made It Myself!

Read...

- Instructions for making fake blood and hairy moles for Halloween.
- Instructions for making a scary Halloween costume.

Link to Literature

- "Best Mask?" a poem by Shel Silverstein.

Objectives:

Reading:

- Following written instructions for making something
- Strategies: Drawing a picture, predicting
- Using illustrations to help you follow instructions
- Literature: Responding to a poem

Writing:

- How-to instructions
- Organizing steps in a time sequence
- Using exact words

Vocabulary:

- Recognizing compounds
- Learning party vocabulary

Listening/Speaking:

- Listening to instructions
- Giving oral instructions
- Giving feedback

Grammar:

- Understanding functions of imperatives

Spelling and Phonics:

- Spelling the /ō/ sound as in *hole* and *boat*

Trick or treat!

BEFORE YOU BEGIN

Talk with your classmates.

1. Look at the picture. Who do you see? Why is he holding his head?
2. Read the caption. What does it mean?
3. What do you know about Halloween? Help your teacher make a list.

A · CONNECTING TO YOUR LIFE

1. Tuning In There's a party at school tomorrow. Listen. What is the teacher doing?

    a. telling a story   b. giving a lecture   c. showing how to do something

2. Talking It Over Juan is getting ready for the party.

Work with a partner. Match the words and phrases on the right with each item in the picture. What kind of party do you think it is?

_____	1. skull mask
_____	2. ghost
_____	3. tombstone
_____	4. carved pumpkin
___*a*___	5. monster mask
_____	6. Halloween costume
_____	7. witch's hat
_____	8. fake teeth
_____	9. fake blood
_____	10. trick-or-treat bag

Read the title of this unit. What do you think this unit might be about? Check (✔) the correct answer.

    _____   1. what to do if you meet a headless man

    _____   2. how to write and follow directions for making things

    _____   3. the history of American holidays

B GETTING READY TO READ

1. Learning New Words Read the following vocabulary words and definitions.

1. **stretch**—to make longer or larger by pulling
2. **cover**—to put something on something else
3. **mix**—to stir together
4. **place**—to put somewhere

5. **have (someone do something)**—to ask (someone to do something for you)
6. **spread**—to push a substance around on a surface
7. **roll**—to make round
8. **remove**—to take out of

Complete the sentences below with the missing vocabulary words. Then write the complete sentences in the correct order to describe how to make a pizza.

1. _____Remove_____ the pizza from the oven when it's bubbly.
2. _____ your dad help you understand the directions.
3. _____ the dough to make a large circle.
4. _____ the dough into a ball.
5. _____ a thin layer of tomato sauce on the dough.
6. _____ the pizza in a 450° oven.
7. _____ flour, salt, yeast, and water in a bowl.
8. _____ the sauce with shredded cheese.

2. Talking It Over Talk with a partner. Imagine that he or she is a visitor from another planet. Give instructions for making or doing something simple that you do every day.

1.

How to brush your teeth

2.

How to make a sandwich

3.

How to boil water

4.

How to give a dog a bath

5.

How to wrap a present

6.

How to . . .

C READING TO LEARN   How-to Instructions

1. Before You Read Imagine that you want to dress up for Halloween. Who or what do you want to be? Work with a partner and talk about your costume.

2. Let's Read You are going to read how-to instructions for making fake blood and hairy moles. As you read, **draw** each step.

Fake Blood

You will need:

- *measuring spoon*
- *a smallbowl*
- *a plasic spoon*

- *3 tabespoons maple syrup*
- *15 drops red food coloring*
- *1 drop green food coloring*

Warning:
Food coloring stains clothes, so dress for a mess

Directions:
a.) Mix the maple syrup and food coloring
b.) Dribble it on your skin and/or lips. (It tastes yummy!)

> Measuring spoons, small bowls, and the plastic spoon are supplies. The maple syrup and food coloring are ingredients.

> Yuck! Why does this fake blood taste yummy?

Hairy Moles

You will need:

- *eyelash glue*
- *1 whole black peppercorn per mole*
- *bristles from a small paintbrush (about 3 per mole)*

Warning: Do not put moles near eyes!

Directions:
a.) Put a dab of eyelash glue on your skin.
b.) Place a peppercorn on the glue spot and hold until glue dries.
c.) Dip one end of a bristle in glue and stick it to peppercorn. Repeat for hairier moles.

> Why do the instructions have this warning?

Source: *National Geographic World*

dribble—to drip in tiny drops

mole—a small dark growth on the skin

dab—a tiny amount

bristle—a hair on a brush

repeat—to do again

3. Unlocking Meaning

❶ Identifying the Purpose Check (✓) the phrase that explains the purpose of the instructions.

_____ 1. to warn you about the dangers of Halloween makeup

_____ 2. to explain how to make Halloween makeup

_____ 3. to teach you how to make a costume

❷ Finding Details Put the steps for making fake blood in the correct order.

_____ Put the blood on your skin.

___1___ Get your supplies and ingredients ready.

_____ Mix the ingredients.

Put the steps for making hairy moles in the correct order.

_____ Glue bristles to the peppercorns.

_____ Hold the peppercorn until the glue dries.

_____ Put the peppercorn on the glue.

_____ Put a tiny drop of glue on your skin.

_____ Get your supplies and ingredients ready.

❸ Think about It Imagine a Halloween party. Fold a piece of paper in four parts to make a chart like the one below. Write a word in each box that explains what you might see at a Halloween party.

1. costumes	3. decorations
Pirate	Jack-o'-lanterns
2. refreshments	4. games or activities
Pumpkin cookies	Bobbing for apples

❹ Before You Move On On Halloween, people dress up as animals, movie stars, ghosts, and other funny or scary things. Do you know about a holiday in another country that is like Halloween? Share what you know with your classmates.

D WORD WORK

1. Word Detective Two nouns can sometimes be put together to form a new noun, called a "compound." Compound nouns have their own meaning:

$$paint + brush = paintbrush$$

You can often understand the meaning of a compound word by looking for the small words inside. Find the small words in each of the following compound words. What does each small word mean? What does each compound word mean? Talk with a partner.

tablespoon	food coloring	shower cap
eyelash	lipstick	sweatshirt
newspaper	tombstone	snowman

2. Word Study There are three types of compound words. Match the types of compound words with the correct examples. Write your answers.

Types of Compound Words

1. Closed compound (one word)
2. Open compound (two words)
3. Hyphenated compound (separated by a hyphen)

Examples

a. life jacket, home run, air conditioning
b. first-class, runner-up
c. bathroom, birthday, eyeball

SPELLING AND PHONICS:
To do this activity, go to page 193.

3. Word Play Complete the chart below. Put each of the following compounds in the correct column. You can use a dictionary.

notebook	~~cardboard~~	nail clipper	hand lotion	potato chip
teaspoon	yardstick	report card	glue stick	hairbrush
hairspray	basketball	textbook	ballpoint pen	tennis racket

making things	playing sports	looking nice	doing schoolwork
cardboard			

E GRAMMAR — Imperatives

1. Listen Up Listen to each sentence. Point your thumb up 👍 if it sounds correct. Point your thumb down 👎 if it sounds wrong.

👍👎 1. Take out your book.

👍👎 2. You open to page 42, please.

👍👎 3. Turn on the oven.

👍👎 4. Please you be quiet during the test.

2. Learn the Rule Read the following rules about imperatives. Then do Activity 1 again.

IMPERATIVES
1. Imperative sentences are used **to give directions**. Leave off the subject *you* in the sentence—start with the verb. *Mix the maple syrup and the food coloring.*
2. Imperative sentences can also be used **to give an order**. Leave off the subject *you*. *Put down your pencils and stop writing.*
3. Imperative sentences can be used **to make polite requests**. Leave off the subject *you*. Use the word *please*. *Shut the door, please.*
4. Finally, imperative sentences can be used **to warn others**. Leave off the subject *you*. *Be careful!*

3. Practice the Rule Read each sentence. Write "D" in front of the sentence if it is part of a set of directions, "O" if it is an order, "R" if it is a request, and "W" if it is a warning.

___O___ 1. Go to the office right now.

_____ 2. Please pass the salt.

_____ 3. Add salt and pepper to taste.

_____ 4. Hand me the scissors, please.

_____ 5. Cut along the dotted line.

_____ 6. Be careful with the scissors.

_____ 7. Discuss it with a partner.

F BRIDGE TO WRITING

How-to Instructions

1. Before You Read Look again at the picture on page 39 at the beginning of this unit. Try to **predict** how Juan made his costume before you read the instructions below.

2. Let's Read Read the instructions below. As you read, write down the things you didn't think of when you were predicting.

Lose Your Head This Halloween

This costume takes a little effort to make, but that's a small price to pay for Halloween greatness.

You will need:
- a flat pece of cardboard 18˝ ✕ 36˝
- wide packing tape
- scissors
- red cloth
- a long raincoat and too-long sweatpants
- someone who will act as an assistant
- a way-too-big shirt
- a marker
- crumpled newspaper
- safety pins

The X is pronounced "by."

Directions:

a. Roll the cardboard into a wide tube and tape it closed.

b. Put it over your head. Have your assistant mark where to cut for your head and shoulders. Remove the tube so your assistant can cut a hole for your head.

c. Stretch tape across the top of the tube to bring the front and back sides closer together/ Cover the top with a red cloth and tape it in place. Put the tube over your head. Make sure it doesn't slump to one side. Poke your head through the hole.

Did you guess right?

d. Pull your way-too-big shirt over the tube and stick your head and hands not your arms through the unbuttoned front. have your assistant button the shirt above and below your head.

e. Tuck the shirt into your too-log sweatpants, which should be pulled up high under your armpits. Have your assistant add the long raincoat. Stuff the sleeves with newspaper and pin them together so it looks as if your hands are coming out of them (see photo). Then "head" out the door to trick-or-treat.

Source: *National Geographic Kids*

assistant—a helper

slump—to fall over

3. Making Content Connections Imagine you are going to attend a Halloween party. What kinds of costumes and make up would you see? Complete the chart below.

Character	Costume	Makeup
1. *A pirate*		
2. *A rock star*		
3. *Cleopatra*		
4. *Werewolf*		
5. **Your choice:** _____		

A rock star

A werewolf

4. Expanding Your Vocabulary Find the word in each row of the following chart that *does not* go with the word in capital letters. Cross out your answers. You can use your dictionary.

a. CELEBRATION	festival	custom	holiday	~~sadness~~	tradition
b. REFRESHMENTS	drinks	prize	appetizers	buffet table	pretzels
c. COSTUMES	mask	wig	makeup	clothes hanger	disguise
d. PARTY GAMES	contest	exercise	competition	prize	winner
e. DECORATIONS	banner	balloons	clothing	streamers	crepe paper

1. Think about It Check (✓) the correct answer. You might read how-to instructions when you—

_____ 1. make a cake   _____ 4. tie your shoes

_____ 2. take a shower   _____ 5. learn a new game

_____ 3. fix a flat tire on   _____ 6. learn to use
your bike   a computer

2. Focus on Organization

❶ How-to instructions have two main parts. The first part lists the **materials** or **ingredients**. The second part lists the **steps** you follow. The steps are in **time order**—the order you do them from beginning to end.

❷ Read how to make "scary scabs." Number the steps in the correct order.

The materials come first.

The steps come next.

Scary Scabs

You will need:
- microwave-safe bowl
- 1 cup cold water
- 1 packet unflavored gelatin
- light corn syrup
- cornmeal
- two small paintbrushes
- dark red lipstick
- safety pins

Directions:

___1___ Mix water and gelatin together in the bowl. Let the mixture stand for two minutes. Microwave on high for 40 seconds. Then let stand for two more minutes until the gelatin dissolves.

_____ Gently tap off excess cornmeal.

_____ Use a paintbrush to gently dab lipstick onto the cornmeal. (Don't press too hard).

_____ Sprinkle a thick layer of cornmeal over the corn syrup. Let it sit for two minutes.

___7___ Use the second paintbrush to gently cover the cornmeal with a thin coating of gelatin.

_____ Place the mixture in the refrigerator until it cools (about 30 minutes).

_____ Slather a thick layer of corn syrup onto your skin in the shape you want the scab to be.

_____ After about 15 minutes, the gelatin will dry, sealing the scab.

Source: *National Geographic World*

cornmeal—ground, dried corn

sprinkle—to scatter tiny pieces

gelatin—a jelly-like substance used in cooking

slather—to spread thickly

corn syrup—a sweet syrup

3. Focus on Style

❶ Look at the following first step. Suppose a set of instructions started with this:

1. Mix ingredients together in the bowl.

What would you put in the bowl? You wouldn't know! Good how-to instructions use **specific words**. Specific words answer questions like these:

- What kind?   **chocolate** milkshake
- How much?   **one cup** of water
- How long?   for **thirty minutes**
- How?   **dribble** butter on your popcorn

❷ Work with a partner. Find examples of exact words in the scary scabs instructions. Make a list.

dark red lipstick _____   _____

_____   _____   _____

❸ Look at the underlined parts of the sentences below. Which specific question does each underlined part answer? Write the letter of a question in each blank.

Questions: _a_   1. Use a <u>microwave-safe</u> bowl.

a. What kind?   _____   2. Add <u>1 cup</u> of water to the gelatin.

b. How much?   _____   3. Microwave on high <u>for 40 seconds</u>.

c. How long?   _____   4. Place the mixture in the refrigerator <u>until it cools</u>.

d. How?

_____   5. <u>Gently</u> dab lipstick onto the cornmeal.

_____   6. Cover the cornmeal with a <u>thin coating</u> of gelatin.

_____   7. <u>After about 15 minutes</u>, the gelatin will dry.

H WRITER'S WORKSHOP How-to Instructions

Write how-to instructions for something you know how to do.

1. Getting It Out

❶ Decide what you will explain. Make a list of things you know how to do. Here are some possibilities.

1.

Making a pizza

2.

Doing a magic trick

3.

Juggling three balls

4.

Making a Halloween mask

5.

Making a book cover

❷ Choose two or three things on your list. Ask yourself the following questions, then decide which activity you will explain to others.

1. How well do I know how to make or do this?
2. How easy/hard is it to explain in words?

Here is how Lori answered these questions. Why did Lori decide to write directions for making a pizza?

Possible things to explain	How well do I know how to make or do this?	How easy/hard is it to explain this in words?
1. *Juggling three balls*	*I know how to do this.*	*Hard to teach with words.*
2. *Making a mask*	*I did this once when I was little.*	*Easy.*
3. *Making a pizza*	*I do this often. I'm good at this!*	*Easy.*

❸ Make a list of the materials or ingredients you will need. Here is Lori's list:

pizza shell	sauce	cheese
mushrooms	onions	pepperoni

❹ Plan your instructions. Think about the steps involved. Put them in **time order**. Here is the "timeline" that Lori made.

1.	2.	3.	4.	5.	6.
Preheat the oven to 350°F.	Slice the mushrooms, onion, and pepperoni.	Remove the crust from package.	Spread the sauce evenly to cover crust.	Spread the ingredients evenly on top of sauce.	Place on pan in oven and bake for 20 minutes.

2. Getting It Down

❶ Turn your timeline into instructions. Complete the planner below.

How to _____

Materials or ingredients:

1. _____   4. _____

2. _____   5. _____

3. _____   6. _____

Warning! (Do you need to warn people about anything?) _____

_____

Directions

1. _____

2. _____

3. _____

4. _____

5. _____

6. _____

❷ Here is what Lori wrote.

Lori lists the ingredients.

How to Make a Pepperoni Pizza

Ingredients

12" pizza pan
pizza crust
bottled sauce

¼ pound mushrooms
1 onion
1 pepperoni stick

She lists the steps in time order.

Directions

1. Preheat oven to 350° F.
2. Slice mushrooms, onion, and pepperoni.
3. Remove pizza crust from package.
4. Spread sauce evenly to cover crust.
5. Spread other ingredients evenly.
6. Place on pan in oven. Bake for 20 minutes or until brown.

She uses specific words.

MINI-LESSON

Using Symbols:
Symbols are often used to stand for certain words:
12" pizza pan = 12-<u>inch</u> pizza pan
350° = 350 <u>degrees</u>
---

3. Getting It Right Take a careful look at what you have written. Use this guide to help you revise your work.

Question to ask...	How to check...	How to revise...
1. Are all of the materials or ingredients listed?	Draw a line to connect each item with the step.	Add any supplies or steps you left out.
2. Did I remember all of the steps? Are the steps in time order?	Imagine that you are actually following each step that you have written.	Add a step if you need to or change the order of the steps.
3. Did I use exact language in each step?	Highlight nouns and verbs that are exact.	Replace general words with words that are exact.

4. Presenting It

❶ Share your instructions with your classmates.

❷ Ask for volunteers to repeat each step in your directions.

❸ As you listen to others, take notes. Use a note-taking guide like this one.

Materials or ingredients needed:

1. _____   4. _____

2. _____   5. _____

3. _____   6. _____

Warnings (if any): _____

Directions:

1. _____

2. _____

3. _____

4. _____

5. _____

6. _____

1. On Assignment Follow the instructions for giving a Halloween party!

❶ Make decorations: Listen to the tape or CD for instructions on making a Jack-o'-lantern. Take notes while you listen. Look at the illustrations to help you understand and remember.

1.    2.    3.

1.    2.    3.

❷ Make and serve refreshments: Make "Eyeball" Cookies.

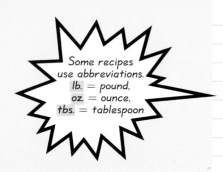

Some recipes use abbreviations.
lb. = pound,
oz. = ounce,
tbs. = tablespoon

Eyeballs

½ cup butter, softened   1½ cups peanut butter
1 lb. confectioner's sugar   1 tbs. vanilla extract
12 oz. white chocolate

1. Cream butter and peanut butter together.
2. Add icing sugar and vanilla. Blend well.
3. Shape into 1-inch balls.
4. Refrigerate on wax paper for one half hour.
5. Melt chocolate. You may use a microwave oven.
6. With a toothpick, dip "eyeballs" into chocolate, covering all but a small circle.
7. Let cool. Makes about 40 eyeballs.

Source: blackdog.net

CONNECT TO THE WEB. CHECK IT OUT:

Go to **www.halloween-online.com**

❸ Play a party game: Draw and Guess! You will need slips of paper with Halloween words like these: *mummy, vampire, haunted house, skeleton, cobweb, witch, jack-o'-lantern, black cat, tombstone, scream, ghost, and bat. Put the slips of paper in a bowl.*

1. Choose two teams or four or five kids.
2. A player on one team takes a slip of paper out of the bowl, then draws a picture of the word.
3. His or her team tries to guess the word in two minutes or less. If they guess the word correctly, the team gets a point.
4. The other team goes next, trying to guess a word.
5. Keep playing until everyone has a chance to draw.
6. Keep score to see which team wins. Give the winners a prize!

2. Link to Literature

🎧 **SHARED READING** People love to wear masks on Halloween. Read "Best Mask?" by Shel Silverstein.

LET'S TALK Answer the questions.

1. What kind of contest did the person in the poem win?
2. Why is the poem funny?
3. Have you ever won a contest? What did you do to win?

BEST MASK?

They just had a contest for scariest mask,
And I was the wild and daring one
Who *won* the contest for scariest mask—
And (sob) I'm not even *wearing* one.

ABOUT THE AUTHOR

Shel Silverstein was born in Chicago, Illinois in 1930 and died in 1999. He wrote many fun stories and poems. Some of his most famous books are *The Giving Tree, Where the Sidewalk Ends,* and *Falling Up.*

4

Trying to Be Cool

Read...

- Stories about teens who did things just to be cool when they were younger.

Link to Literature

- "Motto," a poem by Langston Hughes.

Objectives:

Reading:
- Personal narratives
- Strategies: Questioning the author, predicting
- Literature: Responding to a poem

Writing:
- Writing a personal narrative
- Describing events in a time sequence
- Indentifying your audience: Formal vs. informal language

Vocabulary:
- Using the -er/-or suffix to form nouns from verbs
- Learning words that describe personality

Listening/Speaking:
- Listening to advice
- Comparing different groups of students
- Listening to feedback from others

Grammar:
- Using the simple past tense

Spelling and Phonics:
- Pronouncing words with the letters -gh-

Mr. Cool

BEFORE YOU BEGIN

Talk with your classmates.

1. Look at the picture. Describe the boy.
2. Read the caption. Why is the boy called "Mr. Cool"?
3. What do you know about students who try to be cool?

A CONNECTING TO YOUR LIFE

1. Tuning In Listen to Michelle giving advice. Do you agree or disagree with her advice?

2. Talking It Over

Some things that kids do are cool and some things are not. Look at the pictures below. Are these things cool or uncool?

1.

Shaving your head

2.

Wearing baggy pants

3.

Being mean to friends

4.

Wearing your baseball cap backward

5.

Piercing a part of your body

6.

Carrying a book bag

Work with a partner. Complete the diagram below. Rate the things in the pictures above from 1 (very uncool) to 5 (very cool). Then add three more things.

Very uncool		Pretty cool		Very cool
1	2	3	4	5

Read the title of this unit. What do you think this unit is probably about? Check (✓) the correct answer.

_____ 1. students who are popular

_____ 2. students who did something to be cool but were sorry later

_____ 3. students who did things to stay out of the hot weather

B   GETTING READY TO READ

1. Learning New Words   Read the sentences below. Try to guess the meanings of the underlined words.

1. Everybody at school likes Juan. He's a <u>popular</u> guy.
2. Matt bought an expensive new car to <u>impress</u> the girls.
3. Pedro is great at every sport. He's a real <u>jock</u>!
4. Tom decided to <u>go out for</u> wrestling this season. He always wanted to wrestle.

5. Stefan doesn't care what others think of him. He doesn't care about his <u>image</u>.
6. Most of the girls at school wear <u>brand-name</u> jeans like *BAM!*
7. Marisol still thinks that smoking is "<u>in</u>," but nobody thinks it's cool anymore.
8. Lots of kids do things to be cool, but it often <u>backfires</u> on them instead. They just look silly.

Complete the sentences below with the missing vocabulary words from above.

1. People who are ___*popular*___ have a lot of friends.
2. Kids who love sports often _____ athletic teams like football or track.
3. If something is fashionable, people say it is _____.
4. _____ clothing has a name everybody knows.

5. When you want other people to like you, you might try to _____ them by wearing cool clothes or telling funny stories.
6. Someone who has a positive _____ makes a good impression on others.
7. When you try very hard to impress other people, it sometimes _____.
8. If you love playing sports, people will call you a _____.

2. Talking It Over   Kids in the same social group often look the same, talk the same, and act the same. Work in a small group. Compare two different groups at your school. Complete the following chart.

	Group #1: ___*Jocks*___	Group #2: _____	Group #3: _____
a. How do they dress?	*They wear sports jerseys.*		
b. How do they talk?			
c. What is their image?			

C READING TO LEARN

Personal Narratives

READING STRATEGY

Questioning the Author:

Thinking about questions you might ask the author can help you focus on the information in the reading.

1. Before You Read Think of the things kids do each day to impress other kids. Talk with a partner. Make a list. Share your list with your classmates.

2. Let's Read How far would you go to be "in"? The editors at the magazine *Zillions* asked high school students what they did to be cool in middle-school. Read what they said. As you read, think of a question you would ask each person.

When I was 13, I went out for wrestling. I shaved my head bald so the older wrestlers on the varsity team would think I was cool. It didn't work. They laughed at me and so did kids my age.

—Tom, age 18

When I was 14, I thought my old friends weren't cool enough for me. So I ditched them to impress the cool group. It was stupid and didn't make me popular. I tried to win back my old friends, but it didn't work.

—Robbie, age 18

Why didn't Robbie's friends take him back?

In junior high, I bought only brand-name clothes— "the" clothes to wear. I wanted to impress the popular crowd. It made no difference. The "cool" clique didn't admit members based on clothes. It was stupid to have spent so much for nothing.

—Sarah, age 18

Source: Zillions: CONSUMER REPORTS® for Kids

bald—having no hair on the head

varsity team—the main school sports team

ditch— to get rid of someone

clique—a group that hangs out together

admit— to let someone into a group

3. Unlocking Meaning

❶ Finding the Main Idea Complete the sentences. Match each phrase on the left with the correct ending on the right.

1. Tom learned that—
2. Robbie learned that—
3. Sarah learned that—

a. what you wear won't make other kids like you.
b. changing the way you look to be cool can backfire.
c. if you're not loyal to your real friends, you could end up lonely.

❷ Finding Details Put the following sentences in the same order that they happened in each story.

Tom's Story

_____ He shaved his head bald.

___1___ He joined the school wrestling team.

_____ The other boys laughed at him.

Robbie's Story

_____ He tried to get his friends back but they didn't want him.

_____ He dropped his old friends because he wanted new friends who were cool.

_____ The new group didn't want to be friends with him.

Sarah's Story

_____ She wore brand-name clothes to impress the popular crowd.

_____ She realized that she wasted her money.

_____ The kids in the cool clique weren't impressed.

❸ Think about It Talk with a partner. Decide which person—Tom, Robbie, or Sarah—did the most foolish thing and why. Share with your classmates.

❹ Before You Move On Read this Assyrian proverb: *Tell me your friends and I'll tell you who you are.* List the names of three of your friends. Then write two words that describe each friend. Circle the words that also describe *you*.

D WORD WORK

1. Word Detective Sometimes you can guess what a word means by looking for a smaller word inside the word. The underlined words below are nouns. Find the smaller words inside the nouns. What do the nouns mean? Write down your definitions.

1. Tom is a powerful <u>wrestler</u>.

   smaller word: _____

   definition of "wrestler": _____

   _____

2. I want to be a <u>teacher</u> when I grow up.

   smaller word: _____

   definition of "teacher": _____

   _____

3. Vincent van Gogh was a famous <u>painter</u>.

   smaller word: _____

   definition of "painter": _____

   _____

4. Justin Timberlake is a <u>singer</u>.

   smaller word: _____

   definition of "singer": _____

   _____

5. Who is your favorite <u>actor</u>?

   smaller word: _____

   definition of "actor": _____

   _____

6. Maria is the best <u>player</u> on the team.

   smaller word: _____

   definition of "player": _____

   _____

2. Word Study You can make many verbs into nouns by adding the suffix *-er, -r,* or *-or.* Look at the sentences below. Underline the suffixes.

> **SPELLING AND PHONICS:**
> To do this activity, go to page 193.
> ■ ■ ■

-er/-r/-or = a person who does (something)	
skate	Michelle Kwan is a beautiful **skater.**
act	Tom Cruise is a handsome **actor.**
golf	Tiger Woods is an amazing **golfer.**

3. Word Play Work with a partner. For each of the following verbs, write a noun that means "*someone who…*" Then make a sentence using each noun.

1. write _____   4. visit _____   7. work _____

2. bake _____   5. interview _____   8. drive _____

3. read _____   6. fight _____   9. dance _____

E GRAMMAR   Simple Past Tense

1. Listen Up When you tell a story, you usually use the simple past tense. Listen to each sentence. Point your thumb up 👍 if it sounds correct. Point your thumb down 👎 if it sounds wrong.

👍👎 1. We both leaved our books at school.

👍👎 2. Juan was late for school.

👍👎 3. Tran fix a sandwich for lunch.

👍👎 4. Lourdes turned her homework in late.

👍👎 5. Parveen catched a cold.

👍👎 6. I didn't went to the party.

2. Learn the Rule Learn how to form the past tense. Then do Activity 1 again.

THE SIMPLE PAST TENSE
Use the simple past tense to describe an action or event that took place at a specific time in the past.
1. *Regular* verbs add *–ed* or sometimes *–d* to form the simple past tense. *Maria calls her sister once a week. She **called** her last night.*
2. *Irregular* verbs have simple past tense forms that can be very different from the present tense. Check the dictionary if you're not sure. *Sometimes I leave my books at home. This morning I **left** them on the bus!*
3. When the simple past tense sentence is negative, use the auxiliary verb *did + not*. Do not change the main verb. *I usually don't eat breakfast. I **didn't eat** breakfast this morning.*

Many common verbs are irregular in the simple past tense: be (was/were), have (had), come (came), go (went), give (gave), take (took), speak (spoke), write (wrote).

3. Practice the Rule Write the simple past tense form of each verb below. Underline the irregular verbs.

draw   *drew*   see _____   read _____

help _____   go _____   want _____

eat _____   hear _____   run _____

listen _____   speak _____   walk _____

like _____   do _____   drink _____

F BRIDGE TO WRITING   Personal Narratives

1. Before You Read You are going to read three more stories about stupid things that kids did to be cool. What is one thing you did when you were younger to impress other kids? Share your story with a partner.

2. Let's Read Each story has a title. As you read, use the titles to **predict** what the stories are about.

"Jump on the bandwagon" is an idiom. You have to learn the meaning of the whole phrase to understand it, not just the individual words.

Jumped on the cuffed-pants bandwagon

When I was 13, the "cool" kids cuffed their pants. I jumped on the bandwagon even though most of my pants were a little too short anyway. When I cuffed them, they barely covered my calves. I looked goofy, but at least I had cuffs!
—Jeremy, age 18

Permed my hair

Perms were all the rage in fourth grade. So I got my long, straight, beautiful hair transformed into a short, layered, curly bob. The 'cool' girls were doing weird things with their hair—crimping it, feathering and teasing bangs into a tortured imitation of a celery stalk. It totally backfired on me. I looked like a 9-year-old with 60-year-old hair.
—Tara, age 17

Tara makes her story interesting by using a lot of adjectives and unusual verbs, like transformed and backfired.

Dyed my hair bright orange

When I was 12, it seemed like all the "in" girls had blonde hair. So I used a lightener, and my nice brown hair turned bright orange! I looked like Raggedy Ann and felt really stupid.

—Julie, age 19

Source: *Zillions: CONSUMER REPORTS® for Kids*

cuff—to turn up the bottom of pant legs

jump on the bandwagon—to do what is popular with most people at the moment.

perm—to make hair curly using a chemical treatment

all the rage—very popular

transform—to change completely

tortured imitation—a bad copy

Raggedy Ann—a type of doll with bright red-orange hair

3. Making Content Connections Work with a partner. From the stories you have read, choose the three students you think did the stupidest things to be cool. Check (✔) their names. Summarize their stories by completing the chart below.

For help with summarizing, complete Mini-Unit, Part C on page 190.

☐ Tom   ☐ Sarah   ☐ Julie

☐ Robbie   ☐ Jeremy   ☐ Tara

Name	What they did	Why they did it	What they learned

4. Expanding Your Vocabulary

❶ Everybody has an image. The adjectives below describe a person's image. Match each word on the left with the word on the right that means the same thing or almost the same thing.

1. popular   a. stuck-up
2. mean   b. childish
3. carefree   c. smart
4. intelligent   d. well-liked
5. immature   e. dumb
6. conceited   f. easygoing
7. silly   g. nasty

❷ Is your own image of yourself the same as the image others have of you? Ask three classmates or family members how they would describe you. Complete the following chart.

How I describe myself:	How others describe me:

G WRITING CLINIC — Personal Narratives

1. Think about It A personal narrative is a story about—

□ something that really happened.   □ something funny or embarrassing.   □ something that didn't really happen.

2. Focus on Organization

❶ Personal narratives usually answer three important questions:

1. **What did I do?** *I shaved my head bald.*

2. **Why did I do it?** *I did it so the older wrestlers would think I was cool.*

3. **What was the result?** *Everybody laughed at me.*

Sometimes the story also tells you how the writer felt or what the writer learned.

❷ Now, read two of the stories again. Match each question below with the number of the sentence that answers it.

> ¹When I was 14, I thought my old friends weren't cool enough for me. ²So I ditched them to impress the cool group. ³It was stupid and didn't make me popular. ⁴I tried to win back my old friends, but it didn't work.
>
> —Robbie

___2___ a. What did Robbie do?

_____ b. Why did Robbie do it?

_____ c. What was the result?

> ¹When I was 12, it seemed like all the "in" girls had blonde hair. ²So I used a lightener, and my nice brown hair turned bright orange! ³I looked like Raggedy Ann and felt really stupid.
>
> —Julie

_____ a. What did Julie do?

_____ b. Why did Julie do it?

_____ c. What was the result?

3. Focus on Style

❶ The people who read what you write are called your audience. Choose the statement that describes the audiences for the stories on pages 60 and 64. Check (✓) the correct answer.

_____ 1. They're other students.

_____ 2. They're adults.

_____ 3. They're young children.

❷ Pretend that you wrote two letters about your family vacation—one to a friend, the other to a teacher. Take out a piece of paper. Write *To a Friend* on one side and *To a Teacher* on the other. Then write each sentence below on the correct side of the paper.

1. a. My family always takes really cheap vacations.

   b. My family always takes inexpensive vacations.

2. a. We usually go on vacation in June, when the weather is warm and sunny.

   b. We usually take off in June, when it's nice and hot out.

3. a. We stay clear of any trip that means getting on a plane—my parents are really tightwads!

   b. To save money, my parents prefer taking driving trips.

4. a. My parents drag me along. The idea of me staying at home alone freaks them out.

   b. My parents insist that I come along since they don't want to leave me at home without supervision.

5. a. This year, we piled into our funky old van and drove to a weird place called Water World.

   b. This year, the family climbed into our van and drove to Water World, a popular vacation destination.

6. a. Our vacation was very enjoyable. I can hardly wait for next summer to come!

   b. It turned out that I actually had an OK time. I guess I might agree to go along next summer.

You usually use formal language when you're talking to adults (like your teacher) or to people you don't know.

H WRITER'S WORKSHOP   Personal Narratives

Your class will write a magazine article about dumb things students did when they were younger. Write a paragraph for the article that tells about something *you* did.

1. Getting It Out

❶ Begin by thinking of something you did that was stupid. Maybe you did it to be cool. Or maybe you just did it. Think about these important questions:

1. What did you do?
2. Why did you do it?
3. What was the result?
4. How did you feel about it?
5. Did you learn a lesson?

❷ Plan your story. Make a comic strip that shows what happened. Each square of a comic strip is called a frame. Look at the sample frame below.

❸ Draw the frames in the correct order to tell your story. Use as many frames as you need. Here is the comic strip that Tom drew to help him plan his story.

1. Maybe I'll go out for wrestling. Maybe I'll join the wrestling team.

2. I'm only 13. Maybe I'll look older and tougher if I shave my head!

3. Captions tell what you did.

I found Dad's razor. I shaved my head.

4. Hey! Cool! Jesse Ventura, look out!

5.

6. That was really dumb!

2. Getting It Down

❶ Turn your comic strip into an outline. Use this planner.

> Julie's story is written in a friendly style. It's like she's talking to the reader.

1. What I did: _____

2. Why I did it: _____

3. The result: _____

> Julie tells what she did. She tells why she did it. She describes the result.

❷ Now turn your outline into a paragraph. Here is what Julie wrote:

> Ooops! The verb is in the present tense!

When I was 13, I thought I was really fat. So I went on a diet. I lost ten pounds, but it didn't make me popular. It just made me hungry. All I did was worry about my weight, so I am no fun to hang out with. So instead of dieting, I switched to jogging. I'm much happier now!

MINI-LESSON

Commas with *When*:
If a sentence starts with *when*, use a comma to separate the two parts of the sentence: *When you finish, put everything away.*

---

3. Getting It Right Now take a careful look at what you have written. Use this guide to revise your story.

Questions to ask...	How to check...	How to revise if you need to...
1. Did I tell what I did?	Underline the sentence that tells what you did.	Add details so that the reader knows what you did.
2. Did I tell why I did it?	Circle the sentence that explains why.	Add details that tell the reader your reasons for doing what you did.
3. Did I tell what happened as a result?	Put a star (★) in front of the sentence that tells what the result was.	Add a sentence that describes the result.

4. Presenting It Share your story with your classmates.

1. Show your comic strip to your classmates. Then read your story aloud. Read slowly and speak clearly.

2. Ask if anyone else ever did the same thing. Ask what happened.

3. Ask for feedback from your classmates.

1. On Assignment Imagine that you and your classmates have been asked to submit your stories to kidzstories.com, an online magazine for kids.

Read the menu of links to "Real Life Stories."

❶ Form a group with classmates who wrote stories related to the same link.

❷ Reread your story aloud to your group. As a group, make up a good title for your story.

❸ Using a computer, type your story, then print out enough copies for each person in class.

❹ Collect a story from each of your classmates. Imagine that you are reading their stories on the Web!

SHARED READING Read the poem by famous American poet Langston Hughes. What kind of language does he use?

LET'S TALK Answer the questions.

1. What can you tell about the speaker in the poem?
2. What is the speaker's motto in your own words?
3. What is your own motto? Write it down then share with your classmates.

This is how jazz musicians talk.

ABOUT THE AUTHOR

Langston Hughes was born in Joplin, Missouri, in 1902 and died in 1967. He was famous for writing stories and poems that gave people an idea about true African-American culture.

dig—to like or understand someone or something

jive—jazz music or insincere talk

motto—what somebody believes

in return—by other people

Motto
Langston Hughes

I play it cool
And dig all jive.
That's the reason
I stay alive.

My motto,
As I live and learn,
is: Dig And Be Dug
In Return.

Source: *The Collected Poems of Langston Hughes* by Langston Hughes

Who Eats What

Read...

- A selection about the food chain.

- A report about sea otters disappearing off the west coast of North America.

Link to Literature

- A poem called "Links in the Food Chain."

Objectives:

Reading:
- Following the explanation of a process
- Understanding cause and effect
- Strategies: Taking notes, making a diagram
- Literature: Responding to a poem

Writing:
- Explaining a process
- Making a flow diagram
- Combining sentences with *that* clauses

Vocabulary:
- Using specific terminology
- Learning names for ocean plants and animals

Listening/Speaking:
- Listening to a poem
- Giving examples
- Giving feedback

Grammar:
- Using the present vs. past tense

Spelling and Phonics:
- Spelling the /ōō/ sound as in *food* and *blue*

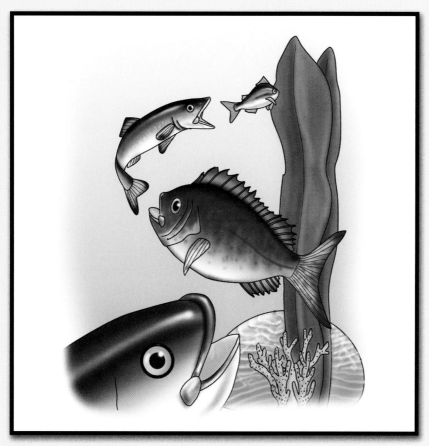

Dinnertime

BEFORE YOU BEGIN

Talk with your classmates.

1. Look at the picture. Describe what you see.
2. Read the caption. Think of another caption for the picture.
3. Why do animals eat other animals?

A CONNECTING TO YOUR LIFE

1. Tuning In Look at the numbered box to the right. Listen to the poem. List each animal in order as you hear its name. How is each animal on your list related to the animal or plant *below* it?

5. _____
4. _____
3. _____
2. _____
1. *flower* _____

2. Talking It Over Work with a partner to answer the question below. Then compare your answer with your classmates' answers.

Question: What kind of relationship does each pair of creatures in this chart have?

Answer: _____

1.

Cat/Mouse

2.

Spider/Fly

3.

Caterpillar/Leaf

4.

Bird/Caterpillar

5.

Shark/Tuna

6.

Human/Chicken

Think again about the answer to the question. What do you think this unit is about?

_____ 1. how plants and animals depend on each other to live

_____ 2. what you will see when you visit the zoo

_____ 3. how mean animals can be to each other

B GETTING READY TO READ

1. Learning New Words Read the sentences below. Try to guess the meanings of the underlined words.

1. Here is the <u>chain</u> of events: Juan made a face, the teacher saw him, she gave him detention.
2. A healthy breakfast gives me <u>energy</u> and strength.
3. Smoking can make you very ill. It <u>causes</u> cancer.
4. It's important to take care of the land, the water, the air, the plants, and the animals—they are all part of our <u>environment</u>.
5. Children can't survive without someone to take care of them. They <u>depend on</u> their parents.

Now match each word on the left with the correct definition on the right.

Children depend on
their parents.

1. chain   a. a source of power or strength
2. energy   b. the natural world around us
3. cause   c. a sequence of closely connected things
4. environment   d. to need and rely on
5. depend on   e. to make something happen

2. Talking It Over Work with a partner. Think about these living things. How are they related to each other?

1.   2.   3.   4.

A squirrel   A grasshopper   A hawk   Grass

 CONNECT TO THE WEB. CHECK IT OUT.

Visit the Smithsonian National Zoological Park at **www.si.edu/natzoo**

Go to the American Library Association's "Great Web Sites for Kids" for links to animal web sites at **www.ala.org**

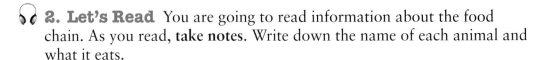

C | **READING TO LEARN** | Explaining a Process

For help with taking notes, complete Mini-Unit, Part B on page 184.

READING STRATEGY

Note-taking:
As you read, you can write down interesting facts or ideas to help you remember them. ■■■

1. Before You Read Talk with a partner. Write the name of an animal. Make a list of the things it eats.

2. Let's Read You are going to read information about the food chain. As you read, **take notes**. Write down the name of each animal and what it eats.

Who Eats What?

1   A caterpillar is eating a leaf on an apple tree. Later the caterpillar is spotted by a wren. It becomes part of the wren's dinner. Still later the wren is eaten by a hawk. Leaf, caterpillar, wren, and hawk are all linked. Together they form a food chain. Each is a link to the chain.

2   The hawk is the top of the food chain because no other animal attacks and eats hawks. The animal at the top of a food chain is always the last eater—the one nobody else eats. Suppose you eat an apple off the tree. That makes you part of a short food chain—the apple and you. You are the top of the food chain. Or suppose you drink a glass of milk. Now you are the top of a slightly longer food chain. The milk came from a cow, and the cow ate the grass. So this chain is grass, cow, you.

3   Food is the fuel our bodies need. Food keeps us alive. It gives us the energy we need to grow, move, and do many other things. The same thing is true for caterpillars, wrens, hawks—for all animals. All must find or catch the foods they need.

4   Every living thing you see is part of at least one food chain. All these food chains begin with green plants. Green plants are the only living things that can make their own food. They are the only living things that do not need to eat something else.

5   Green plants take energy from sunlight. They use it to make food out of water and air.

6   All animals depend on green plants for food, even animals that don't eat plants. Hawks, for example, do not eat green plants. But the hawk ate the wren that ate the caterpillar that ate the leaf of a green plant. And so the hawk is linked to green plants through the food chain. It needs the plants as much as the caterpillar does.

Source: *Who Eats What? Food Chains and Food Webs* by Patricia Lauber

This is called a flow diagram.

caterpillar—an early stage of a butterfly; like a hairy worm

wren—a type of tiny bird

hawk—a type of meat-eating bird similar to an eagle

fuel—something that helps create energy

3. Unlocking Meaning

❶ Finding the Main Idea Which of the following statements says what the reading selection is mostly about? Check (✔) the correct answer.

_____ 1. All animals need food to live.

_____ 2. Animals are linked to other animals and plants through the food chain.

_____ 3. Some animals eat both plants and other animals.

❷ Finding Details

1. Number the following events in the correct order.

_____ Hawks eat wrens.

_____ Caterpillars eat leaves.

_____ Wrens eat caterpillars.

2. Read the sentences below. Write *T* for *True* and *F* for *False*.

__F__ 1. Animals at the bottom of the food chain are safe from other animals.

_____ 2. Human beings are at the bottom of the food chain.

_____ 3. Food gives our bodies energy.

_____ 4. All food chains begin with insects.

_____ 5. Green plants take their energy from the soil.

_____ 6. All animals eat some type of green plants.

_____ 7. All animals are linked to green plants through the food chain.

❸ Think about It Talk with a partner. Imagine that there are no more green plants on earth. What would happen to hawks? Why?

❹ Before You Move On Work in a small group. Make a "food chain" for the ingredients in a cheeseburger.

1. Make a list of the ingredients in a "typical" cheeseburger.
2. Circle one ingredient.
3. Write what the ingredient depends on for energy.

lettuce ◄— sun

4. Draw a food chain for the ingredient. Include yourself at the top of the food chain.

D WORD WORK

1. Word Detective Match each name with a picture.

    _e_   1. golden retriever   _____   5. rattlesnake

  _____   2. black bear   _____   6. yellow jacket

  _____   3. praying mantis   _____   7. German shepherd

  _____   4. vampire bat   _____   8. hammerhead shark

a.

b.

c.

d.

e.

f.

g.

h.

SPELLING AND PHONICS:
To do this activity, go to page 194.
---

2. Word Study You can make some nouns more specific by adding another word. For example, many animals have names that explain where they come from, what they look like, or what they do.

WHERE IT COMES FROM OR LIVES	WHAT IT LOOKS LIKE	WHAT IT DOES
saltwater crocodile	hammerhead shark	killer whale

3. Word Play Make a chart like the one in Activity 2. Look at the animal names in Activity 1. Decide what each name tells you and put it in the correct place on the chart. Some animals may fit in more than one place.

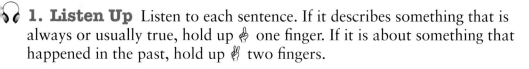

E GRAMMAR   Present Tense vs. Past Tense

1. Listen Up Listen to each sentence. If it describes something that is always or usually true, hold up 👆 one finger. If it is about something that happened in the past, hold up ✌️ two fingers.

 1. Caterpillars eat leaves.

 4. Green plants take energy from sunlight.

 2. The wren ate the caterpillar for dinner.

 5. The spider caught the fly in its web.

 3. All food chains begin with green plants.

 6. Hawks do not eat green plants.

2. Learn the Rule Read these rules for when to use the present and past tenses, then do Activity 1 again.

PRESENT TENSE VS. PAST TENSE
1. When you want to talk about things that are always or usually true, use the *present tense*.
*Most cats **eat** mice.*   *The sun **comes** up every morning.*
2. When you want to talk about an event that happened in the past, use the *past tense*.
*The cat **ate** the mouse that it **caught** under the house.*   *We **saw** a full moon last night.*

3. Practice the Rule Complete each sentence below with the correct form of the verb in parentheses.

1. Many animals (eat/ate) _____*eat*_____ plants for their food.
2. Plants (use/used) _____ energy from the sun.
3. The hawk was hungry. He (eats/ate) _____ the mouse.
4. Food (gives/gave) _____ our bodies energy.
5. The shark (attack/attacked) _____ the swimmer. It tore him in two.
6. In the early 1800s, cowboys (kill/killed) _____ nearly all the buffalo.
7. Wrens (are/were) _____ one of a hawk's favorite foods.
8. Hawks never (eat/ate) _____ plants. They only eat animals.

F BRIDGE TO WRITING   Explaining a Process

1. Before You Read Look again at the flow diagram on page 78. What do you think might happen if the wren disappeared from the food chain? What would happen to the caterpillars? What would happen to the green plants?

---READING STRATEGY---
Making Diagrams:
Making a diagram can help you understand what happened to someone or something in a story or an article.
■ ■ ■

2. Let's Read This article describes what happened when people killed so many sea otters that they almost disappeared completely. As you read, **make a diagram** that shows what happened to the otter.

> Why do you think the kelp, eagles, harbor seals, and fish disappeared?

Humans often make changes in food chains. Then they find that one change causes other changes. That was what happened when hunters killed nearly all the Pacific sea otters.

² The otters lived off the west coast of North America. They lived in beds of giant seaweed, called kelp. Every year thousands of otters were killed for their fur. By the early 1900s almost none were left. But as the otters disappeared, so did beds of kelp. And so did eagles, harbor seals, and fish. What had happened? The answer lay in the kelp.

³ Kelp is a green plant at the start of many food chains. It is eaten by tiny animals that are eaten by bigger animals that are eaten by fish. The fish are food for eagles and seals, as well as people.

⁴ Kelp is also eaten by spiny animals called sea urchins. In eating, they may cut off stems at the seafloor. The kelp then floats away.

⁵ Sea urchins are one of the foods otters like best. But when hunters killed the otters, there was no one to eat the urchins. The urchins destroyed the kelp beds.

⁶ Once the hunting stopped, the otters made a comeback. They ate sea urchins, and the kelp began to do well. When the kelp did well, the fish came back—and so did the eagles, seals, and fishermen.

> Sea otters are still endangered. What do you think that means?

Source: *Who Eats What? Food Chains and Food Webs* by Patricia Lauber

---

seaweed—a family of underwater ocean plants

destroy—to put an end to

3. Making Content Connections Work with a partner. Complete
the chart below.

	On land	In the sea
a. Give an example of an animal at the top of a food chain.		
b. Give an example of a plant at the bottom of a food chain.		
c. Name an animal that eats only plants.		
d. Name an animal that eats other animals.		

4. Expanding Your Vocabulary Food chains in the sea are hard
to study because the plants and animals live underwater. Match the words
and phrases in the box with each item in the picture.

_____ 1. kelp   _____ 7. squid

___e___ 2. mackerel   _____ 8. tuna

_____ 3. octopus   ___h___ 9. anchovy

_____ 4. killer whale   _____ 10. seal

_____ 5. red algae   ___g___ 11. sea lion

_____ 6. krill   _____ 12. herring

G WRITING CLINIC

Explaining a Process

1. Think about It You would probably find a magazine article about the food chain in—

☐ Mad   ☐ Teen People   ☐ Science and Nature

2. Focus on Organization

❶ Reread the first paragraph.

A caterpillar is eating a leaf on an apple tree. Later the caterpillar is spotted by a wren. It becomes part of the wren's dinner. Still later the wren is eaten by a hawk. Leaf, caterpillar, wren, and hawk are all linked. Together they form a food chain. Each is a link to the chain.

This **flow diagram** shows how the food chain works. Flow diagrams use lines and arrows to show how things happen. Look at the diagram. What does a hawk eat?

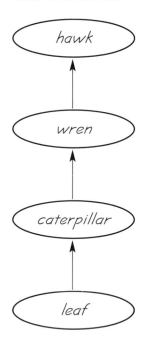

❷ Read again about sea otters on page 82, then make a flow diagram like this one. Where are sea otters in the ocean food chain?

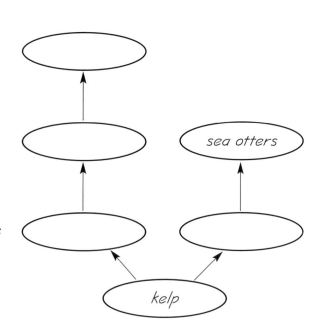

❸ What happened when the sea otters disappeared? Complete the following diagram.

| 1. Hunters killed almost all the sea otters. |

⬇ *so...*

| 2. There were no sea otters to eat the _____. |

⬇ *so...*

| 3. There were so many sea urchins that they destroyed the _____. |

⬇ *so...*

| 4. Tiny sea animals didn't have _____ to eat. |

⬇ *so...*

| 5. Bigger fish didn't have _____ to eat. |

⬇ *so...*

| 6. Eagles and seals didn't have _____ to eat, so they disappeared. |

3. Focus on Style

❶ Writers sometimes combine two sentences when they have the same noun. The new sentence has a clause with the relative pronoun *that*.

The hawk ate the wren.   The wren ate the caterpillar.

The hawk ate the wren that ate the caterpillar.

This is like a "sentence chain!"

❷ Combine each pair of the following sentences to make one sentence.

1. The cat ate the mouse.   The mouse ate the cheese.
   The cat ate the mouse that ate the cheese.

2. The dog chased the cat.   The cat ate the rat.
   _____

3. The wren ate the caterpillar.   The caterpillar ate the leaf.
   _____

4. The hawk ate the wren.   The wren ate the caterpillar.
   _____

H WRITER'S WORKSHOP   Exploining a Process

Imagine that *Kids Discover* magazine has invited your class to write short articles about the food chain.

1. Getting It Out

❶ Learn more about food chains on land and in the sea. Check out these fact files. Find food chains. Choose one food chain to write about.

Fact file: Animals on land

Animal	What it eats
1. beetle	flowers, leaves, fruit
2. cricket	leaves
3. snail	leaves
4. chipmunk	berries, acorns, snails, crickets
5. rabbit	tree bark, vegetables
6. weasel	rabbits, mice
7. coyote	rabbits, sheep
8. hawk	chipmunks, smaller birds

Fact file: Animals in the sea

Animal	What it eats
1. krill	algae, kelp, sea lettuce
2. anchovy	algae, kelp, sea lettuce
3. herring	algae, kelp, sea lettuce
4. squid	krill
5. tuna	krill, anchovies, herring, sardines
6. sea lion	herring
7. shark	tuna, mackerel
8. killer whale	sea lions

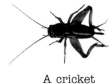

A cricket

A snail

A rabbit

A weasel

❷ Use a large sheet of paper and colored markers. Draw a flow diagram that shows the food chain you have chosen. Use arrows to show who eats what. IMPORTANT: Save your flow diagram for later.

Here is a diagram that Zaida drew to show a food chain in the ocean:

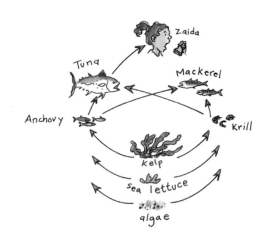

CONNECT TO THE WEB. CHECK IT OUT.

For information about food chains, go to the Forest Service Web Site at **www.fs.fed.us**

❸ Think about why your food chain is important. Ask yourself questions like these:

1. Where do I fit into this food chain?
2. How do all animals connect to green plants?
3. What would happen if one animal or plant disappeared from this food chain?

2. Getting It Down

❶ Turn your flow diagram into words. Use the outline below.

1. Lead sentence: _____.

2. Description of the food chain

   a) At the bottom of the food chain: _____.
                            (1)

   b) Who eats (1): _____.
                    (2)

   c) Who eats (2): _____.
                    (3)

   d) Who eats (3): _____.
                    (4)

3. What is important to understand about the food chain: _____

_____.

❷ Turn your outline into a short article. Here is what Zaida wrote.

> The article has a good lead sentence.

> The information is accurate and matches Zaida's flow diagram.

> Zaida uses combined sentences with words like *that*.

All sea creatures eat other sea creatures and plants to survive. Algae and plants like sea lettuce and kelp are at the bottom of the food chain. Many types of fish and animals such as krill and anchovy eat sea plants.

Larger fish, like tuna and mackerel, eat the smaller animals and fish that eat sea plants.

And who eats the tuna? The next time you eat at a seafood restaurant, check out the menu! You might find tuna there!

> The ending is clever. Zaida shows how human beings are part of the food chain! That's important to understand.

MINI-LESSON

Using Commas:
Put commas around examples:
Correct: Huge fish, like sharks, eat tuna.
Incorrect: Huge fish like sharks eat tuna.

---

3. Getting It Right Take a careful look at what you have written. Use these questions to help you review and revise your work.

Questions to ask...	How to check...	How to revise...
1. Did I name each plant or animal in the food chain?	Circle each animal. Then draw a line to what it eats.	Add any information that is missing.
2. Did I describe the food chain accurately?	Look up each animal in the encyclopedia or the Fact File to check what it eats.	Correct the information, if necessary.
3. Did I put the information in the right order?	Check to see that the information in your article matches your outline.	Correct the information, if necessary.
4. Did I show that I understand why the food chain is important?	Underline the part that shows that you thought about the food chain.	Add a sentence or two that shows your own thoughts about the food chain.

4. Presenting It Present your article to your classmates. Take notes as you listen to other students.

❶ Plan your presentation. Look at the checklist.

❷ Begin by showing your classmates the flow diagram you made to show the food chain.

❸ Read your article aloud.

❹ Invite your classmates to ask questions.

❺ Ask for feedback from your classmates on your presentation.

<table>
<tr><td colspan="2">Presentation Checklist</td></tr>
<tr><td>☐</td><td>The information is accurate.</td></tr>
<tr><td>☐</td><td>The information that is presented flows well.</td></tr>
<tr><td>☐</td><td>The flow diagram is carefully drawn and labeled and is easy to understand.</td></tr>
<tr><td>☐</td><td>The speaker uses a loud, clear voice.</td></tr>
<tr><td>☐</td><td>The speaker pauses briefly after each idea.</td></tr>
<tr><td>☐</td><td>The speaker looks up at the audience from time to time.</td></tr>
</table>

❻ As you listen to each presentation, take notes. Use a note-taking guide like this:

Animal	What it eats
krill	*algae, kelp*
What is important to understand about the food chain:	

❼ Using your notes, volunteer to describe your classmate's presentation about food chain in your own words.

1. On Assignment Imagine that you are an animal. To survive, you must convince your classmates that you are important to the environment.

❶ Pretend you are one of these animals.

1.

A grasshopper

2.

A hawk

3.

A field mouse

4.

A caterpillar

5.

A garter snake

6.

A fox

7.

A cricket

8.

An owl

9.

A chipmunk

10.

A frog

❷ Visit your school or community library. Find out—

1. what you are like and where you live.
2. what you eat and what eats you.
3. why you are valuable in the environment.
4. what would happen if you and all your species were destroyed.

❸ Present a short report to your classmates.

1. Describe yourself and where you live.
2. Tell what you eat and what eats you.
3. Explain how the food chain would be damaged if you disappeared.
4. Give reasons why you should survive.

2. Link to Literature

🎧 **SHARED READING** Listen to this happy poem about the food chain. Then read it aloud.

LET'S TALK

1. In the poem, what is at the top of the food chain? What is at the bottom?

2. Why is the poem fun to listen to and to say aloud?

3. Would the poem be more interesting or less interesting if it ended with the line where the finger is pointing? Why?

> *Anonymous means that the author's name is unknown.*

Links in a Food Chain
By Anonymous

¹ There once was a fox, and I'll make a bet:
He'd eat anything he could possibly get.

² The fox ate the snake, who often grabbed birds,
And swallowed them whole, or so I have heard.

³ The snake ate the bird, who gobbled up bugs,
And creepies and crawlies, and slimies and slugs.

⁴ The bird ate the bug, who nibbled on flowers,
Nibbled on flowers for hours and hours!

⁵ The bug ate the flower that grew on the plain,
Where the sun helped it grow, and so did the rain—
Links in the food chain.

⁶ The fox he grew older and died one spring day,
But he made the soil rich, when he rotted away.

⁷ A new flower grew where he died on the plain.
And the sun helped it grow, and so did the rain—
Links in the food chain.

> *This is an example of alliteration. The same sounds are repeated.*

> *This is an example of words that rhyme. Are there any more?*

Unit 6

Real-Life Heroes

Read...

■ A story about a young girl who saved a man in danger.

■ A story about four boys who survived a bear attack.

Link to Literature

■ "Paul Bunyan and the Gumberoos," a story by Steven Kellogg.

Objectives:

Reading:
■ Reading stories about real-life heroes
■ Identifying elements of plot
■ Strategy: Predicting
■ Literature: Responding to a tall tale

Writing:
■ Writing a true adventure story
■ Taking interview notes
■ Writing titles and leads

Vocabulary:
■ Forming compounds that come from sentences
■ Learning words for accidents and emergencies

Listening/Speaking:
■ Listening to real-life stories
■ Comparing stories
■ Interviewing others

Grammar:
■ Using adverbial time clauses

Spelling and Phonics:
■ Pronouncing words with the letters -oo-

Attack and rescue!

BEFORE YOU BEGIN

Talk with your classmates.

1. Look at the picture. What is the animal in the picture?
2. Read the caption. What do you think is happening?
3. What would you do in this situation?

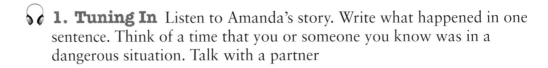

A **CONNECTING TO YOUR LIFE**

🎧 **1. Tuning In** Listen to Amanda's story. Write what happened in one sentence. Think of a time that you or someone you know was in a dangerous situation. Talk with a partner

2. Talking It Over Match the headlines with the pictures.

Headlines are usually in the present tense.

_____ b _____   1. Boy Saves Girl in Boating Accident

_____   2. Local Girl Rescues Child Who Falls in Underground Tank

_____   3. Girl Saves Drowning Pet; Pulls Animal from River.

_____   4. Teen Drives Bus to Safety

_____   5. Boy Pulls Child from Railroad Tracks; Tragedy Avoided

_____   6. Seventh-grader Aids Tornado Victim

a.

b.

c.

d.

e.

f.

What do you think this unit is about? Check (✔) the correct answer.

_____   1. kids who were afraid to help

_____   2. kids whose pictures were in the newspaper

_____   3. kids who saved other people's lives

B GETTING READY TO READ

1. Learning New Words Read the following vocabulary words and definitions.

1. **save a life**—to stop someone from dying
2. **hero**—someone who is very brave, especially who risked his/her life
3. **rescue**—to save from danger
4. **stay calm**—to avoid getting too excited
5. **emergency**—a serious situation that needs immediate action
6. **first aid**—emergency help for an injured person
7. **paramedic**—someone trained to give medical help in an emergency
8. **tragic**—causing terrible destruction or death

Complete the sentences below with the new vocabulary words.

1. Ashley dialed 911. "This is a(n) ___emergency___," she cried. "My baby brother fell into the swimming pool!"
2. When you _____, you often get your name in the paper.
3. Tom jumped into the lake to _____ his dog.
4. Boy Scouts and Girl Scouts are trained to give _____.
5. The _____ saved Mr. Johnson's life when he had a heart attack.
6. Tran escaped from the burning car. He avoided a(n) _____ accident.
7. If you see an accident, don't cry. Try to _____.
8. That firefighter saved my life. He is a(n) _____!

2. Talking It Over Can you remember a time when you or someone you know was in danger? What happened? Tell a partner. Be ready to share your partner's story with your classmates.

1. Before You Read Look at the picture that goes with the following story. Before you read, **predict** what happened. Tell the story in your own words. Talk with a partner.

2. Let's Read You are going to read a true story about Ashley Makale, an average teen who became a real-life hero. After you read the first sentence, stop and try to predict what will happen.

Calm under Pressure

1 When Ashley Makale took a Red Cross baby-sitting class, she had no idea the skills she learned would someday save a life. But that's exactly what happened. Ashley was baby-sitting for neighbor Barry Becker's three-month-old daughter and five-year-old son while Becker worked at home. When Becker ran to stop his dog from chasing a cat in the backyard, he crashed through a sliding-glass door.

> Compare the first sentence in the story and the last sentence. What do you notice?

2 *Fast call.* Ashley saw Becker fall and rushed to his side. He had deep gashes in his knee and foot. Becker was losing so much blood that Ashley knew she had to get help and stop the bleeding fast. Holding the baby, Ashley ran to the phone and dialed 911. Then she used a towel to apply pressure to Becker's knee while she reassured the children. Paramedics soon arrived. After several surgeries, Becker began long-term physical therapy to use his leg again.

> Notice how the details make the story interesting.

3 *Real lesson.* Ashley was honored by the Los Angeles County Sheriff's Department for her actions. "I didn't know everyone would think this was such a big deal," Ashley says. "That baby-sitting class taught me to stay calm in an emergency, and that's just what I did."

Source: *National Geographic World*

---

pressure—(1) urgent problems; (2) pressing hard on something

Red Cross—an organization that helps injured people or disaster survivors

reassure—to give comfort

physical therapy—special treatment for injuries to the body

3. Unlocking Meaning

❶ Finding the Main Idea Which of these sentences tells the most important idea from the article? Check (✓) the correct answer.

_____ 1. Glass doors are very dangerous.

_____ 2. A girl took a baby-sitting class from the Red Cross.

_____ 3. A girl saved a man's life by staying calm during an emergency.

❷ Finding Details Number the sentences in the order that they happened in the story.

___1___ Ashley took a baby-sitting class.

_____ Ashley tried to stop Becker's bleeding.

_____ Becker ran through a sliding-glass door.

_____ The paramedics arrived.

_____ Ashley saw that Becker was bleeding a lot.

_____ The Sheriff's Department honored Ashley.

_____ Becker fell and Ashley ran to his side.

_____ Ashley called 911 to report the emergency.

❸ Think about It What do you think happened **after** the paramedics arrived? Number the following sentences in the order you think they happened.

_____ The paramedics drove Becker to the hospital.

_____ The paramedics gave Becker first aid.

_____ Becker had surgery.

_____ The paramedics put Becker in the ambulance.

_____ Becker spent several days in the hospital.

❹ Before You Move On People who do brave things sometimes receive a special certificate to honor them. Design a certificate to honor Ashley. Use the certificate to the right as an example. Explain what she did on the certificate.

Real-Life Heroes **97**

D WORD WORK

A frying pan

1. Word Detective Match each compound word in the left-hand column with its correct meaning on the right.

1. baby-sitter   a. a place where you can catch a bus
2. life-saving   b. a machine for cutting grass
3. frying pan   c. someone who cares for a young child
4. dishwasher   d. saving someone's life
5. bus stop   e. something you use for cooking
6. lawnmower   f. a machine for washing dishes

2. Word Study Many compounds are made from a verb + a noun. You can often figure out what a compound means by making a sentence that explains it. Notice that the noun and verb switch places in many compounds.

SPELLING AND PHONICS:
To do this activity, go to page 194.

VERB + NOUN (DIRECT OBJECT)	
1. A barber gives **haircuts**.	A barber cuts hair.
2. The president gave me a **handshake**.	The president shook my hand.
VERB + NOUN (OBJECT OF A PREPOSITION).	
3. They're **machine-made**.	The toys were made by a machine.
4. John is a **factory worker**.	John works in a factory.

3. Word Play Read the sentences on the left. Complete each sentence on the right with a compound word.

1. Ana makes dresses.   Ana is a __dressmaker__.
2. We both like riding on horseback.   We both like horseback _____.
3. The furniture is made by hand.   The furniture is _____ made.
4. The cowboys on TV are fighting with guns. The cowboys on TV are having a gun _____.
5. Ms. Sanchez makes pizza.   Ms. Sanchez is a pizza _____.

E | GRAMMAR   Adverbial Time Clauses

1. Listen Up Listen to each sentence. Point your thumb up 👍 if it sounds correct. Point your thumb down 👎 if it sounds wrong.

👍 👎 1. After he put on his seat belt, he got in the car.

👍 👎 2. The Chang family was eating dinner when the doorbell rang.

👍 👎 3. Wipe your feet on the mat before you walk in the house.

👍 👎 4. I was playing basketball while I fell and broke my arm.

2. Learn the Rule Read the following rules for adverbial time clauses, then do Activity 1 again.

ADVERBIAL TIME CLAUSES		
When, while, before, and *after* link one event to another event. Clauses that start with these words are called adverbial time clauses. An adverbial clause can come before or after a main clause.		
when	(at the specific point that something else happened) *When* Clause: first event Main Clause: second event	*When Becker fell, Ashley ran to his side.* *Ashley ran to Becker's side when he fell.*
while	(at the same time that a longer continuing event was happening) *While* Clause: continuing event Main Clause: short event	*While I was eating, the phone rang.* *The phone rang while I was eating.*
before	(before something else happened) *Before* Clause: second event Main Clause: first event	*Before you arrived, I cleaned the house.* *I cleaned the house before you arrived.*
after	(after something else happened) *After* Clause: first event Main Clause: second event	*After we ate dinner, I washed the dishes.* *I washed the dishes after we ate dinner.*

3. Practice the Rule Complete the following sentences. Use *when, while, before,* or *after.*

1. I was watching TV _____*when*_____ the phone rang.
2. _____ the alarm went off, I jumped out of bed.
3. The alarm went off _____ I was sleeping.
4. _____ I took a shower, I got dressed.
5. I ate breakfast _____ I left for school.
6. Mary turned on the radio _____ she got into the car.
7. My parents came home _____ I was taking a nap.

F BRIDGE TO WRITING   True Stories

─READING STRATEGY─
Predicting:
When you predict, you use things like pictures and titles to help you guess what you're going to read about.
■■■

1. Before You Read This story is about a camping trip. Think of one or two problems you might have on a camping trip. Share them with a partner.

🎧 **2. Let's Read** Look at the picture and read the title and the subheadings of the following story. **Predict** what the story is about. Talk with a partner.

"BEAR-LY" IN TIME

¹ Every summer brothers Joey and Ryan L'Heureux and their cousins Jonathan and Kerry look forward to Boy Scout camp. But last year's camping trip with fellow Scout Matt Murphy almost turned tragic.

> Why is the first paragraph a good lead?

² *TEAMWORK.* One morning the boys heard something outside their tents. "When I looked out, I saw a black bear crashing into Matt's tent—with Matt inside!" says Joey. Kerry and Joey ran to get Matt's dad while the other boys tried to distract the bear. The bear dragged Matt and his tent down a ravine.

> The quoted words make the story a lot more exciting to read.

³ *RACE FOR HELP.* When Matt's dad arrived, he was able to chase the bear up a tree while Jonathan and Ryan pulled Matt out of the tent. Then Jonathan ran to the camp's first aid station to call for help. The other boys stayed with Matt until the paramedics arrived. Though he had scalp wounds and cuts requiring 195 stitches, Matt is fine today.

⁴ *REWARD.* The four L'Heureux boys received the Boy Scouts' Lifesaving Award Honor Medal. "Matt needed our help," says Jonathan, "and we did what we had to do."

Source: *National Geographic World*

distract—to make someone pay attention to something else

ravine—a deep, narrow valley

3. Making Content Connections Work with a partner. Compare the two stories you have read in this unit. Then complete the following chart, using your own words.

	Calm Under Pressure	"Bear-ly" in Time
1. Who are the people in the story? Circle the name of the hero or heroes.		
2. Where did the story happen?		
3. What happened? What was the emergency?		
4. What actions did the hero or heroes take?		
5. How did the story end?		

4. Expanding Your Vocabulary Match the emergency on the left with the correct action to take on the right. You can use your dictionary to look up the underlined words.

_f_   1. You sprain your ankle.

_____ 2. Your little sister drinks liquid soap, thinking that it's milk.

_____ 3. Your mother cuts her hand.

_____ 4. Your friend is bitten by a strange dog that has no collar.

_____ 5. Your brother falls and scrapes his knee.

_____ 6. You are stung by a bee.

a. Read the <u>label</u> for what to do.

b. Take the person to the <u>emergency room</u>.

c. Apply a thin layer of <u>antibiotic</u> cream.

d. Apply <u>pressure</u> to the wound with a clean cloth.

e. Gently scrape out the <u>stinger</u> with a blunt object (like a credit card).

f. Apply a cold <u>compress</u>.

G WRITING CLINIC — True Stories

1. Think about It You would probably read a true story in—

☐ a history book.   ☐ a magazine.   ☐ an encyclopedia.

2. Focus on Organization Read the story, "Calm under Pressure" again. Notice how the story is organized.

Calm under Pressure

Paragraph 1

LEAD: These sentences set the scene. You can tell something is going to happen!

→ When Ashley Makale took a Red Cross babysitting class, she had no idea the skills she learned would someday save a life. But that's exactly what happened.

This sentence tells you what was happening *just before* the accident.

→ Ashley was babysitting for neighbor Barry Becker's three-month old daughter and five-year-old son while Becker worked at home.

ACTION: This sentence describes the accident.

→ When Becker ran to stop his dog from chasing a cat in the backyard, Becker crashed through a sliding-glass door.

Paragraph 2

These sentences describe the rescue. They tell what Ashley did.

→ Ashley saw Becker fall and rushed to his side. He had deep gashes in his knee and foot. Becker was losing so much blood that Ashley knew she had to get help and stop the bleeding fast. Holding the baby, Ashley ran to the phone and dialed 911. Then she used a towel to apply pressure to Becker's knee while she reassured the children.

This sentence describes how the rescue ended.

→ Paramedics soon arrived.

ENDING: These sentences tell how everything turned out.

→ After several surgeries, Becker began long-term physical therapy to use his leg again.

Paragraph 3

Ashley was honored by the Los Angeles County Sheriff's Department for her actions.

Ashley's words tell us how she felt about the experience.

→ "I didn't know everyone would think this was such a big deal," Ashley says. "That baby-sitting class taught me to stay calm in an emergency, and that's just what I did."

3. Focus on Style

❶ Interesting stories often have creative titles. Look again at the titles of each reading. Explain how the title relates to the story.

Example: *Calm under Pressure—Ashley didn't panic in an emergency and she saved a man's life.*

❷ For each story on the left, choose the best title from the column on the right. Work with your classmates.

1. A boy saves his brother, who is trapped under the bed when a twister hits.
2. A boy rescues a girl in a boating accident.
3. A girl rescues a child from a fast-approaching train.
4. A girl rescues a child who falls into an underground cave.
5. A boy stops a school bus that is out of control.
6. A boy helps his mother give birth to a baby because she can't get to the hospital.

a. On the Right Track
b. Tornado Terror
c. Help! I'm Drowning!
d. It's a Boy!
e. It's Cold and Dark Down Here!
f. Step on the Brake!

A railroad track

Stepping on the brake

❸ Good stories also have leads that set the scene for what is going to happen. Match each lead on the left to the best title on the right.

1. The sky turned black. Tim heard a roar. It was a twister!
2. Doctors learn to deliver babies in medical school. But Vincent Cho learned how before the eighth grade!
3. When the bus driver slumped over the wheel of the bus, Danny Johnson knew he had to act—and act fast!
4. "I'm being sucked into the ground!" screamed Ana.
5. Most summer days, Juan and his friends spend their time boating on Lake Wobegon.
6. Shannon Smith's heart stopped when she heard the train's roar and the child's screams.

a. On the Right Track
b. Tornado Terror
c. Help! I'm Drowning!
d. It's a Boy!
e. It's Cold and Dark Down Here!
f. Step on the Brake!

For help with taking notes, complete Mini-Unit, Part A on page 182.

H **WRITER'S WORKSHOP**   True Stories

Imagine that you have been asked to write a story for a book called *Kids Did It! Real-Life Heroes*.

1. Getting It Out

❶ You will listen to two interviews with people who helped others in danger. Take notes. You will use your notes from the second interview to write your story.

❷ Read the interview questions.

Interview Questions

1. Who was involved?

2. Where did the incident happen?

3. What happened?

4. How did everything turn out?

5. How did you feel?

❸ Listen to the first story. Practice taking notes.

❹ Here are the notes that Stefan took. Compare your notes with his.

Story #1: Interview Questions

1. **Who was involved?** *Karla Pierce and family members, dog Tucker.*

2. **Where did the incident happen?** *In my backyard, which has a stream running behind it.*

3. **What happened?** *My family was having a barbecue in backyard with friends. Suddenly, someone shouted that our dog Tucker had fallen in the stream. The stream was moving really fast. I rushed to the edge of the stream and could see that Tucker was in trouble. He was fighting the current and kept hitting rocks. So I stretched out on the bank (it was really slippery!) and hooked my foot around a tree. I reached out over the water and grabbed Tucker by the paw. I pulled him out of the water. (He weighs 100 pounds.)*

4. **How did everything turn out?** *We were both cold, muddy, and wet but were OK.*

5. **How did you feel?** *I was really scared. I knew that if I didn't do something, Tucker might drown. Sometimes you have to try your hardest and not give up, you know.*

❺ Now listen to the **second story. Take** notes. Use Stefan's notes as an example. You will use **these notes to** write your real-life story.

2. Getting It Down

❶ Turn your interview notes into an outline for your story. Use the story planner below.

One way to give your story a good title is to use an adjective and noun that start with the same letter—like "Terrifying Tornado."

MINI-LESSON

Using Exclamation Points:
You can use an exclamation point at the end of a sentence to show excitement or strong emotion:
I won!

TITLE: _____

LEAD:

People and setting: _____.

ACTION:

1. The problem: _____.

2. What happened next:

    a. _____.

    b. _____.

    c. _____.

ENDING:

1. How the story ended: _____.

2. How the person felt: _____.

❷ Turn your outline into a story. Here is what Stefan wrote:

The title is clever!

Stefan does a good job describing the situation and how Karla rescues her dog.

Dog Catcher

Karla Pierce and her family were hosting a barbecue in the backyard for friends. Several dogs were playing together. Suddenly someone yelled, "Tucker's in the stream!"

Karla dashed to the water's edge. "I could see that Tucker was fighting the current and hitting rocks," says Karla. The eighth-grader stretched out on the muddy bank and hooked her foot around a tree. Hanging out over the water, she grabbed Tucker by the front paw and pulled the hundred-pound dog up the steep bank. Though muddy, wet, and cold, both

were unharmed.

"At the time, I wasn't scared. I knew if I didn't do

something, Tucker might drown," says Karla. "Sometimes

you have to try your hardest and not give up."

> The ending is strong. Karla shares the lesson she learned.

3. Getting It Right Now take a careful look at what you have written. Use these questions to help you revise your story.

Questions to ask...	How to check...	How to revise...
1. Does my story have a strong lead?	Underline the sentence(s) that set(s) the scene.	Add words that explain what was happening just before the problem occurred.
2. Did I describe the problem?	Put two stars (★★) before the sentence that describes the problem.	Add words that describe the problem.
3. Did I say what happened in time order?	Put a star (★) before each event.	Add sentences that explain what happened in time order?
4. Did I describe how the problem was solved?	Put a wavy line under the sentence that says how the problem was solved.	Add a sentence that describes how the problem was solved.
5. Does my story have an exciting ending?	Highlight the ending.	Add a sentence that says how everything turned out. Add a quote that describes a lesson learned or how someone felt.

4. Presenting It Read your true story to your classmates.

❶ Begin by giving a brief introduction to the story. Say the names of the people involved in the story and where it took place.

❷ Share the title.

❸ Read your story slowly and clearly. Whenever a person in the story talks, say their words just the way they would say them in real life.

1. On Assignment Choose a "Citizen of the Month" for your class. Have an award ceremony to honor that person.

❶ As a class, brainstorm the qualities that a Citizen of the Month should have.

❷ Nominate a classmate. Explain why you are nominating that person.

Qualities of a Citizen of the Month

- Comes to class on time
- Brings books and other things to class
- Listens and takes notes
- Participates in class activities
- Works well with others
- Does all homework

I nominate Lori because she always pays attention.

❸ If more than one person is nominated, make a ballot with the top three names. Vote for the Citizen of the Month.

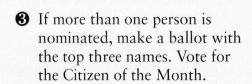

❸ Choose a classmate with good writing to make a Certificate of Honor for the chosen person.

❺ Have an award ceremony. Congratulate the winner! Tell the winner why he or she won.

I'd like to congratulate Lori for being chosen Citizen of the Month. Lori always comes to class ready to learn. Here is your certificate, Lori. Congratulations.

2. Link to Literature

🎧 **SHARED READING** All cultures have stories about fictional heroes who did great things. Paul Bunyan is a famous fictional hero in an American story. According to the story, Paul Bunyan and his giant blue ox, Babe, created the Grand Canyon and the Black Hills of South Dakota! Read about one of Paul Bunyan's adventures. As you read, look for examples of **exaggeration** (making something seem bigger, stronger, or better than it really is).

LET'S TALK

1. Write down an example of exaggeration.
2. What is the effect of exaggeration on the story?
3. All cultures have legends. Do you know a story about a legendary hero?

ABOUT THE AUTHOR

Steven Kellogg was born in Norwalk, Connecticut in 1941. He started writing when he was a young boy, and has written almost 90 books.

Paul Bunyan and the Gumberoos

¹   At seventeen, Paul grew a fine beard, which he combed with the top of a pine tree.
²   By this time, other settlers were beginning to crowd into the Maine woods. Paul felt an urge to move on. He said good-bye to his parents and headed west.
³   Paul wanted to cross the country with the best lumbering crew available. He hired Ole, a celebrated blacksmith, and two famous cooks, Sourdough Slim and Creampuff Fatty. Then he signed up legendary lumbermen …
⁴   On the far slopes of the Appalachian Mountains, several of Paul's men were ambushed by a gang of underground ogres called Gumberoos.

⁵   Paul grabbed the camp dinner horn and blew a thunderous note into the Gumberoos' cave, determined to blast the meanness right out of them.
⁶   To Paul's dismay, the Gumberoos responded by snatching the entire crew. A wild, rough-and-tumble rumpus began inside the den.
⁷   When the tussle was over, the Gumberoos needed six weeks to untangle themselves. They disappeared into the depths of the earth, and they've never been heard from again.

Source: *Paul Bunyan* by Steven Kellogg

settler—someone who moves into a new region

lumbering crew—workers who cut down trees

blacksmith—someone who makes things with iron

Appalachian Mountains—a chain of mountains running from Canada to Alabama

ambush—to make a surprise attack

ogre—a monster that often eats people

Gumberoos—made-up creatures

dismay—disappointment

rumpus/tussle—a fight

into the depths of the earth—deep under the ground

Nature's Fury

Read...

- A terrifying description from "Twister: Winds of Fury."

- A firsthand account of the San Francisco earthquake in 1906.

Link to Literature

- "The Turtle Tale," a myth about why earthquakes happen.

Objectives:

Reading:

- Reading first- and third-person descriptions of events (natural disasters)
- Strategy: Visualizing
- Literature: Responding to a myth

Writing:

- Describing an event: An eyewitness account
- Writing paragraphs with a topic sentence and facts
- Using action-packed verbs
- Using similes

Vocabulary:

- Recognizing synonyms
- Learning sensory words

Listening/Speaking:

- Listening to an eyewitness report
- Comparing two disasters

Grammar:

- Reviewing the past tense

Spelling and Phonics:

- Pronouncing words with the letters -ou-

Earthquake!

BEFORE YOU BEGIN

Talk with your classmates.

1. Look at the picture. What do you see?
2. Read the caption. Why is the ground cracked?
3. Were you or someone you know ever in an earthquake? What was it like?

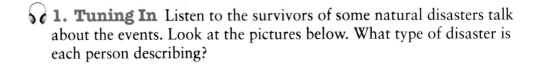

🎧 **1. Tuning In** Listen to the survivors of some natural disasters talk about the events. Look at the pictures below. What type of disaster is each person describing?

2. Talking It Over Work with a partner. Look at the photographs below. Which natural disaster would you fear most? Give one or more reasons.

Can you remember a natural disaster in your own life or one you heard about? Write one or two sentences that explain what happened.

EXAMPLE: *I lived through an earthquake. The house shook. Dishes fell off the shelves.*

1.

An earthquake

2.

A hurricane

3.

A flood

4.

A wildfire

5.

A tornado

6.

A tsunami

Read the title of this unit. What do you think this is probably about? Check (✓) the correct answer.

_____ 1. what to put in a disaster survival kit

_____ 2. what it is like to experience a natural disaster

_____ 3. what scientists are doing to predict natural disasters

B GETTING READY TO READ

1. Learning New Words Read the sentences below. Try to guess the meanings of the underlined words.

1. Every building was destroyed by the earthquake. The <u>demolished</u> buildings were just dust.
2. The buildings all fell down. There was nothing but piles of <u>rubble</u>.
3. The walls of our house fell, then the roof. The entire house was <u>flattened</u>.
4. The wind blew hard, then stopped. We were glad when it <u>subsided</u>.
5. The earthquake was very powerful. When the first <u>shock</u> hit, it knocked me out of bed!
6. As usual, I got up at 7, took a shower, and ate breakfast. It was a <u>normal</u> morning.
7. Suddenly, we heard a terrible <u>rumble</u> from the ground. That sound told us it was an earthquake!

Now match each word on the left with the correct definition on the right.

1. demolished   a. typical or usual
2. rubble   b. a strong jolt
3. flatten   c. a deep, rolling sound
4. subside   d. completely destroyed
5. shock   e. to die down or become less
6. normal   f. to knock down to the ground
7. rumble   g. crumbled rock, bricks, etc.

2. Talking It Over Imagine that you lived through a disaster. Work with a partner. Choose one disaster. Talk about what it was like then complete the following chart.

	What did you see?	**What did you hear?**	**How did you feel?**
1. Earthquake	*I saw houses falling down.*	*I heard …*	*I felt …*
2. Tsunami			
3. Hurricane			

C READING TO LEARN

Describing an Event

1. Before You Read You are going to read a description of a tornado. Look at the source at the bottom of the reading. What do you think another name for a tornado is?

☐ twister ☐ hurricane ☐ wildfire

2. Let's Read As you read, **visualize** what's happening in the story. What would be the most frightening part?

I Survived a Tornado!

1 For Carson Birch of Hesston, Kansas, it started as "just a normal evening" in 1990, when he was 7 years old.
2 My mom and four sisters and I were all sitting around eating pancakes and getting ready to go to a school program. Then we heard sirens going off. We looked out one window, and the sky was totally clear. But my mom looked out the other direction and it was really black.
3 We decided to go down to the basement, where my bedroom was. Then the electricity went out, and my mom got scared. We got onto my bunk beds, covered up with cushions from the couch, and all sang a hymn.
4 You could hear this rumbling noise, like a big train, It got louder and louder and louder. We couldn't even hear ourselves sing. And all of a sudden, in a second, it stopped. The tornado was gone.
5 We went upstairs and tried the door to the kitchen, but it wouldn't open. The ceiling had fallen in on the kitchen! The door to the garage was open, so we went outside. Some of the houses were gone. There were just cement slabs with people coming out of them, from down in their basements. Pretty soon my dad got home from his store, which had been flattened. It's amazing that in our whole town no one died from the tornado. I remember seeing a car up in a tree, But the strangest thing was that a week after the tornado I was in a park and found a half-broken Nintendo game that said "Birch" on it. It was ours! The tornado had carried it clear across town.
6 After that we wore shirts that said "*I SURVIVED THE BIG ONE.*" Now I'm 14, and the tornado is the only thing I can remember about the first grade!

Source: "Twister: Winds of Fury," from *National Geographic World*

siren—a piece of equipment on police cars and fire engines that makes very loud warning sounds

bunk beds—two beds that are attached, one on top of the other

hymn—a religious song

slab—a thick piece of something hard, like cement

3. Unlocking Meaning

❶ **Finding the Main Idea** Which of the following statements is the main idea of the story? Check (✓) the correct answer.

_____   1. Tornadoes are scarier than earthquakes.

_____   2. Tornadoes can be both dangerous and destructive.

_____   3. Tornadoes move round and round.

❷ **Finding Details** Number the sentences below in the order that they happened in the story.

_____   Carson's mother saw that part of the sky is black.

_____   The family heard a loud rumbling noise.

___1___   Carson and his family were eating dinner.

_____   The tornado moved on.

_____   Sirens went off.

_____   Carson remembers the tornado.

_____   Carson and his family went down to the basement.

_____   The family learned their home was damaged.

_____   Carson's father came home.

_____   Carson found his Nintendo game in the park.

❸ **Think about It** Based on the reading, what are two important safety rules to follow during a tornado? Check (✓) the best answers.

_____   1. Go to the basement or a room on the lowest floor.

_____   2. Get in your car and try to run away from the tornado.

_____   3. Get up on the roof of your house.

_____   4. Move away from windows.

❹ **Before You Move On** The Fujita Scale measures the force of tornadoes in **miles per hour** (MPH). Read the following descriptions, then decide which type of tornado hit Rob's farmyard.

Fujita Scale		
F-0	Gale (40–72 MPH)	damages chimneys
F-1	Moderate (73–112 MPH)	peels off shingles
F-2	Significant (113–157 MPH)	rips off roofs
F-3	Severe (158–206 MPH)	flips over cars
F-4	Devastating (207–260 MPH)	destroys houses
F-5	Incredible (261–318 MPH)	carries buildings far away

D WORD WORK

1. Word Detective Match the words in the left column with the words on the right that mean the same (or almost the same) thing.

1. noisy		a.	boom
2. bang		b.	blow up
3. dark		c.	loud
4. throw		d.	black
5. fear		e.	twist
6. swirl		f.	peaceful
7. explode		g.	toss
8. quiet		h.	be afraid

2. Word Study Words that mean the same thing are called *synonyms*. Knowing synonyms can help you choose just the right word. Synonyms usually have slightly different meanings. Depending on the sentence, you might prefer to use one word rather than another.

SPELLING AND PHONICS:
To do this activity, go to page 195.

silent	*Two minutes later, all was <u>silent</u>.*
quiet	*I need a <u>quiet</u> place to study.*

3. Word Play Work with a partner. Find a more interesting synonym for each underlined word. You can use a dictionary or a thesaurus.

1. We heard a <u>loud</u> noise.

2. Clouds were <u>turning</u> in the sky.

3. The tornado <u>touched</u> the ground.

4. Windows <u>broke</u>.

5. The winds <u>pulled</u> off the roof.

6. We were <u>afraid</u>.

E GRAMMAR
Review: Simple Past Tense

1. Listen Up Listen to each sentence. Point your thumb up 👍 if it sounds correct. Point your thumb down 👎 if it sounds wrong.

👍 👎 1. We heared the sirens go off.

👍 👎 2. It began to rain and hail.

👍 👎 3. The wind blowed hard.

👍 👎 4. We went down to the basement.

2. Learn the Rule Learn how to use the past tense. After you have learned the rules, do Activity 1 again.

THE SIMPLE PAST TENSE	
1. Use the simple past tense to describe an action or event that took place at a specific time in the past. Form the simple past tense of regular verbs by adding –ed or -d.	Suddenly the sky turned black. Thunder rolled and lightening flashed.
2. Remember that many common verbs are irregular: come (came), go (went), be (was/were), have (had), and make (made). Check the dictionary if you are not sure.	Right: The windows blew in. Wrong: The windows blowed in.

3. Practice the Rule Look at this Pennsylvania boy's eyewitness report. Complete the sentences with the past tense forms of the verbs in the box.

say	notice	get	come	appear
~~look~~	know	be	run	jump

My Tornado Story

It started as a regular day. I ___looked___ out the window and _____ dark, black clouds. I _____ to myself, "OK—it's nothing to worry about." Ten minutes later, a thunder cloud _____ in the distance. The wind _____ stronger and was coming from the southeast at about 45 to 50 miles per hour. I _____ really worried.

It started to hail and rain really hard. I saw a funnel. I _____ what that meant: it was a tornado! The clouds swirled around. The tornado _____ closer! I _____ outside and _____ into a ditch about five feet deep. I'm thankful I'm alive after that close call!

F BRIDGE TO WRITING   Describing an Event

1. Before You Read An eyewitness is someone who sees something happen. Have you ever been an eyewitness to an event? What did you see?

2. Let's Read On April 18, 1906, a terrible earthquake hit San Francisco. Thomas Jefferson Chase was walking to work. This is his eyewitness account. As you read, **visualize** Chase's journey.

Square brackets [] tell you that these are not the writer's words.

Marks like these … tell you that words have been left out.

1 The morning was clear and bright, not a breath of air was stirring. The city was asleep. The time was 5:18, morning of April 18th, 1906…

2 I usually walked down Folsom to First, [then] to Market Street to eat before going to work.

3 I had reached about halfway to Howard on the west side of First Street when I heard a low distant rumble. … I stopped and listened. Then it hit.

4 Power and trolley lines snapped like threads. The ends of the power lines dropped to the pavement …, writhing and hissing like reptiles. Brick and glass showered about me.

5 Buildings along First Street from Howard to Market crumbled like card houses. One was brick. Not a soul escaped. … The dust hung low over the rubble in the street.

This story is told in the first person. The narrator is telling a story about himself.

6 [When] this shock stopped, I crossed over to the east side of the street. As soon as I reached the curb a second shock hit. This was harder than the first. I was thrown flat, and the cobblestones danced like corn in a popper. More brick and glass showered down on the sidewalk.

7 As soon as it subsided, I started for Howard Street. By the time I reached the corner, a third shock hit. I was under the old Selby Shot Tower. I expected to see it go but it didn't. The flagpole on the building whipped and snapped like the popping of a whip.

8 I started down Howard for the Ferry. Looking down First Street through the dust of demolished buildings a wisp of black smoke was rising through the dust. …

9 [When I finally reached the Embarcadero], the entire south wall of the Ferry Building was out. It crashed down into the Bay. The waves were lazily lapping at the pilings as if nothing had happened.

Source: sfmuseum.org

trolley—a streetcar

cobblestone—a paving stone

piling—a heavy beam that supports a building at the water's edge

3. Making Content Connections You have read about two kinds of disasters that can strike. Work with a partner. Complete the chart below.

	Tornado	Earthquake
1. What sights and sounds do you hear?	*dark sky*	
2. What kind of damage can it cause?		
3. Why is it so dangerous to people?		

4. Expanding Your Vocabulary

❶ Your writing can be more exciting to read if you use verbs that are "action packed":

Everyday verb: Juan *got* under the table.
Action-packed verb: Juan *leaped* under the table.

❷ Rewrite the sentences below. Use an "action-packed" verb from the box. Make sure you put the new verbs in the past tense.

snap	~~jump~~	swirl	sway
crash into	rip off	tumble over	shatter

1. Juan <u>got</u> under a table. _____ *jumped* _____
2. The clouds <u>moved round and round</u> in the sky. _____
3. The winds <u>took off</u> the roof from the house. _____
4. The buildings <u>moved back and forth</u>. _____
5. The skyscraper <u>fell.</u> _____
6. The bridge <u>broke</u> in two. _____
7. The car <u>hit</u> the tree. _____
8. The windows <u>broke</u> into tiny pieces. _____

G | WRITING CLINIC

1. Think about It When you describe an event, you want your readers to—

☐ feel like they are there   ☐ laugh   ☐ feel sad

2. Focus on Organization Learn how to describe an event.

❶ A description of an event has three parts.

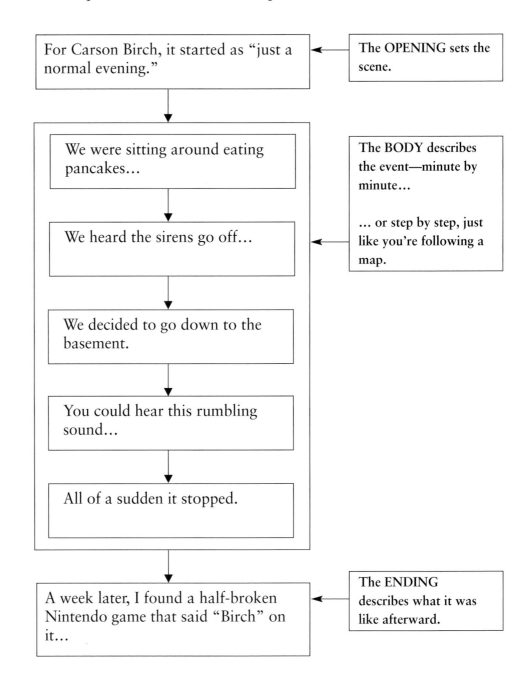

For Carson Birch, it started as "just a normal evening."	The OPENING sets the scene.

We were sitting around eating pancakes…

We heard the sirens go off…

We decided to go down to the basement.

You could hear this rumbling sound…

All of a sudden it stopped.

The BODY describes the event—minute by minute…

… or step by step, just like you're following a map.

A week later, I found a half-broken Nintendo game that said "Birch" on it…	The ENDING describes what it was like afterward.

❷ Reread the eyewitness report of the San Francisco earthquake. Make your own "map" that shows how each event happened.

3. Focus on Style

❶ A good description provides details about how things look, sound, feel, taste, or smell. Reread the description of the earthquake. Make a chart like this one. Include as many sights, sounds, feelings, tastes and smells as you can in the chart.

sight	sound
writing like reptiles	*low, distant rumble*
feel	**taste/smell**
Not a breath of air was stirring . . .	*no examples*

❷ The writers of both readings in this unit use figurative language—words and phrases that "paint a picture" for the reader. These sentences all use *similes*. Similes compare two things that are not usually compared to each other.

The word like tells you that a simile follows.

1. Mud and grass swirled up like smoke from a bonfire.
2. Power and trolley lines snapped like threads.
3. Cobblestones danced like corn in a popper.
4. The clouds bubbled at the top like boiling milk.
5. Buildings crumbled like card houses.

❸ Make up your own similes. Complete each of the following sentences.

1. The huge clouds spun like _____.
2. The tornado moved toward us like _____.
3. The earthquake made a noise like _____.
4. The building shook like _____.
5. The dishes in the cupboard rattled like _____.
6. The breaking windows sounded like _____.
7. The bridge collapsed like _____.

H WRITER'S WORKSHOP
Describing an Event

Imagine that your class is writing a book called "Mother Nature's Anger." You will write an eyewitness account that describes an event.

1. Getting It Out

❶ Imagine what it would be like to live through a natural disaster. As you look at the following photos, what images come into your mind?

❷ Choose one natural disaster to write about. What words describe what it is like? Complete the chart below with words that describe the feelings, sounds, and sights of the event.

	Looked like. . .	Sounded like. . .	Felt like. . .
1.			
2.			
3.			

❸ Maria decided to write about an earthquake. She recreated the event in "slow motion":

1.

2.

3.

❹ Here is what Maria wrote about an earthquake. Add to her chart below.

Looked like. . .	Sounded like. . .	Felt like. . .
1. Trees started to shake.	I heard a rumble.	I felt the ground under me move.
2. I saw cracks in the roads.	The rumble got louder—like a jet engine.	The shaking knocked me to the ground.
3. Cars turned over. Buildings fell down.	It was deathly quiet.	

2. Getting It Down

❶ Use your diagram to make an outline of the event.

Title: _____

1. Before the event: _____.

2. The event:

   A. What happened: _____.

     Sights: _____.

     Sounds: _____.

     Other sensations: _____.

   B. What happened: _____.

     Sights: _____.

     Sounds: _____.

     Other sensations: _____.

3. After the event: _____.

---

❷ Turn your outline into a paragraph or two. Here is what Maria wrote:

> It was a day like any other day. I was walking home from school. I was at the top of Potrero Hill, where I could see the city below. Suddenly, I heard a low rumble. Trees started to sway. I felt the ground under my feet begin to shake. It was an earthquake!
>
> The shaking became more violent. Cracks opened up in the roads, buildings began to crumble like cookies, and cars veered off the road like pieces on an overturned chessboard. The roar grew louder, like a huge jet flying over the city.
>
> After 30 long seconds, the shaking stopped. A picture of deadly destruction lay before me—toppled buildings, huge cracks in the earth, and cars thrown about like a child's toys.

— MINI-LESSON —

Combining Sentences:
When several short sentences are combined into one, they are separated by commas:

Cracks opened up the roads, buildings began to crumble, and cars veered off the road.

∎∎∎

❸ Evaluate Maria's eyewitness account:

1. Copy the sentences that set the scene.
2. Copy the sentences that describe what happened during the earthquake.
3. Copy examples of figurative language.
4. Copy the sentences that describe what it was like right after the earthquake ended.

3. Getting It Right Take a careful look at what you have written. Use these questions to help you review and revise your work.

Questions to ask...	How to check...	How to revise...
1. Do I set the scene?	<u>Underline</u> the sentences that set the scene.	Add a sentence or two that says what was happening right before the disaster hit.
2. Does my report make the reader feel they were there?	Ask a neighbor if your report helps them imagine the event.	Add more details. Use action-packed verbs that show, not tell.
3. Do I use sensory language?	Circle the words and phrases that relate to the senses.	Add more sensory details. Describe the sights and sounds of the event.
4. Do I use figurative language?	Draw a box around words that are examples of figurative language.	Add a simile or two to your report.
5. Does my ending describe the aftermath?	Draw a wavy line under the ending.	Add a sentence that describes the scene or tells how people felt after the event.

4. Presenting It Share your eyewitness report with your classmates.

❶ Read the title of your report.

❷ Begin by reading the part that sets the scene. Read clearly and calmly.

❸ Next read your description of the disaster. Use your voice to express the excitement of the event.

❹ Ask your classmates for feedback on your report.

1. On Assignment Imagine that a tornado has hit your town! You are reporting live from the scene for your school's cable TV program, Channel 55 Eyewitness News. You will have a 45-second spot to tell your story.

❶ Look over the scene. Take notes on the damage.

❷ Figure out how you will start your story. Your lead must grab the attention of your viewers, or they will switch the channel!

a. *I'm standing in front of the ruins of an office building downtown!*

b. *The damage from yesterday's tornado is unbelievable!*

c. *Many buildings were destroyed, but incredibly no one was hurt!*

❸ Write your story. Describe the destruction. Use sensory details. Keep in mind the "Four Cs" of good news stories:

Be current.   **Be correct.**   **Be concise.**   **Be clear.**

❹ Present your story to your class. Speak slowly, calmly, and clearly. Look into the camera!

2. Link to Literature

A myth is a very old story about why the world is the way it is.

SHARED READING Different cultures try to explain nature in different ways. Read this myth about earthquakes.

LET'S TALK

1. Find examples in this myth that make it fun to read.
2. In many myths, who are the main characters?
3. Do you know a myth about the Earth that you can share?

Great Spirit—God

straw—dried wheat stems

restless—not able to keep still

beast—a wild animal

argue—to disagree with someone

every once in a while—sometimes

The Turtle Tale

¹ Long, long ago, before there were people, there was hardly anything in the world but water. One day, Great Spirit looked down from heaven. He decided to make a beautiful land. But where could he begin? All he saw was water. Then he spotted a giant turtle. Great Spirit decided to make the beautiful land on the turtle.

² But one turtle was not big enough. The land Great Spirit wanted to make was very large. So he called out, "Turtle, hurry and find your six brothers." …. After six days, turtle had found her six brothers. "Come," she said, "Great Spirit wants us."

³ Great Spirit called down. "Turtles! Form a line, all of you—head to tail, north to south…. What a beautiful land you turtles will make! Now listen! It is a great honor to carry this beautiful land on your backs. So you must not move!"

⁴ The turtles stayed very still. Great Spirit took some straw from his supply in the sky. He spread it out on the turtles' backs. Then he took some soil and patted it down on top of the straw.

⁵ Great Spirit cleaned his hands on a fluffy white cloud. Then he went to work, shaping mountains and valleys, and lakes, and rivers. When he was finished he looked at the beautiful land he had made. Great Spirit was very pleased. But soon trouble came. The giant turtles grew restless. They wanted to stretch their legs. "I want to swim east," said one. "This beast goes east." "West is best. I'll swim toward the setting sun," said another.

⁶ The turtles began to argue…. One day, four of the turtles began to swim east. The others began to swim west. The earth shook! …. But after a minute, the shaking stopped. The turtles had to stop moving because the land on their backs was so heavy…. When they saw that they could not swim away, they stopped and made up.

⁷ Every once in a while, though, the turtles argue again. Each time they do, the earth shakes.

Source: *California Geology Magazine*

Drugs: The True Story

Read...

- Pamphlets that persuade you that drugs and tobacco are dangerous.

- Facts about common drugs and tobacco—and why people who use them take such big risks.

Link to Literature

- A selection from *Go Ask Alice*, the real diary of a fifteen-year-old who died from drugs.

Objectives:

Reading:

- Reading informational text that persuades
- Identifying the elements of persuasive text (opinion statements, reasons, facts, and examples)
- Strategies: Identifying the main purpose, skimming
- Literature: Responding to a diary entry

Writing:

- Writing persuasively
- Supporting a position with facts and examples
- Using questions to guide and organize writing

Vocabulary:

- Learning prefixes that mean "not": *non-, il-, in-, dis-*
- Learning words that describe the effects of drugs and tobacco

Listening/Speaking:

- Listening to dialog
- Comparing two places
- Giving feedback

Grammar:

- Using gerunds as subjects and objects

Spelling and Phonics:

- Pronouncing words with the letters *-ea-*

Three Teens Killed in Drunken Driving Accident

Talk with your classmates.

1. Look at the picture. What happened?
2. Read the headline. Why did the accident happen?
3. What do you know about drinking beer and alcohol?

A CONNECTING TO YOUR LIFE

1. Tuning In Listen. What is Amy trying to do? Check (✓) the correct answer.

_____ 1. She's explaining to Maria why alcohol is dangerous.

_____ 2. She's trying to make Maria drink alcohol.

_____ 3. She's telling Maria why they shouldn't drink alcohol.

2. Talking It Over

❶ Write one reason that using drugs, alcohol, or tobacco can be dangerous. Share your reason with a partner.

alcohol   drugs   tobacco

❷ Here are some possible facts about alcohol, drugs, and tobacco. Talk with a partner. Decide which statements *might* be true and which *might* be false. Circle your answers.

True False 1. About 3,000 kids start smoking every day.

True False 2. Most teens (over 80 percent) do NOT use tobacco.

True False 3. Nearly half of all teens have tried an illegal drug at least once.

True False 4. Smoking causes almost 90 percent of all lung cancer.

True False 5. Illegal drugs are always dangerous.

True False 6. Most hard drug (cocaine, heroin) users started with marijuana.

True False 7. If you're caught with a drug, you could go to jail.

❸ Read the title of this unit. What do you think is the main idea of the unit? Check (✓) the correct answer.

_____ 1. Many kids don't know the names of drugs.

_____ 2. Many kids don't understand that drugs can be harmful.

_____ 3. Many kids don't know people who take drugs.

B GETTING READY TO READ

1. Learning New Words Read the sentences below. Try to guess the meanings of the underlined words.

1. Even one beer changes the way you see or do things. It <u>affects</u> your behavior.
2. Tobacco can cause many problems with your body. It is harmful to your <u>health</u>.
3. Smoking can make your lungs weak and sick. It can <u>damage</u> them.
4. Smoking kills people. That's 100% true—it's a <u>fact</u>!
5. People who <u>abuse</u> drugs are foolish.
6. Tran is telling Stefan not to smoke. He is trying to <u>persuade</u> him that smoking is bad.
7. Using certain drugs can kill you—they can be <u>fatal</u>.

Complete the sentences below with the new vocabulary words.

1. Tobacco can make you sick. It is very bad for your ____*health*____.
2. A _____ is something that is completely true.
3. When one thing _____ something else, it means that one thing causes a change in the other.
4. Something that causes death is _____.
5. It can _____ your eyes if you look directly at the sun.
6. When you use something in a way it should not be used, you _____ it.
7. When you try to _____ someone, you give them good reasons for doing—or *not* doing—something.

2. Talking It Over Work in a small group. Draw a chart like this one and complete it. Talk about the ways that harmful drugs affect people's lives.

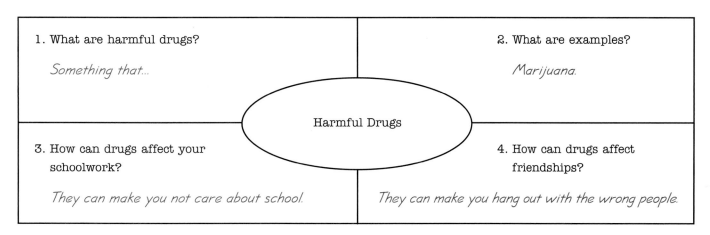

1. What are harmful drugs?

   Something that...

2. What are examples?

   Marijuana.

Harmful Drugs

3. How can drugs affect your schoolwork?

   They can make you not care about school.

4. How can drugs affect friendships?

   They can make you hang out with the wrong people.

C | READING TO LEARN — Persuasive Writing

1. Before You Read You are going to read a brochure about drugs and alcohol. But first, read the first sentence of the brochure. What do you think the main idea is?

2. Let's Read As you read, try to **identify the purpose** of the brochure.

- ☐ to entertain the reader
- ☐ to persuade the reader
- ☐ to tell the reader a story

---

¹ *People who abuse drugs and alcohol take big risks. Some aren't aware of the risks. Others believe that bad things only happen to other people. The truth is that abusing drugs and alcohol can—*

DAMAGE HEALTH

> Think of one more example of how drugs might affect someone's performance.

² Any drug that is abused can damage physical and mental health. Drugs can affect your brain, affect your heart, and damage other parts of your body like your liver, lungs, and kidneys. Some drugs can put you in a coma and can even cause sudden death.

INTERFERE WITH PERFORMANCE

³ Certain drugs affect concentration, memory, attitude, and other skills needed in the classroom and on the athletic field. They can affect the way you move, react to situations, think, hear, and see.

HURT RELATIONSHIPS

> What does "create a wall" mean in this sentence?

⁴ Drug abuse can create a wall between the abuser and his or her family and friends. Imagine a life in which drugs are more important than the people you love.

> The last paragraph is the closing. Why does the brochure end this way?

⁵ The risks of drugs and alcohol multiply in certain situations! Mixing alcohol with other drugs, such as tranquilizers, increases the risk of death. Sharing needles to inject drugs increases the risk of getting fatal illnesses such as AIDS. Using hard drugs can cause permanent loss of brain function!

DO YOU STILL WANT TO DO DRUGS?

Source: Coalition for a Drug-Free City

---

risk—the chance something bad could happen

coma—a deep sleep that you can't come out of

performance—the act of doing something

permanent—lasting forever

brain function—how the brain works

3. Unlocking Meaning

❶ **Finding the Main Idea** Choose the best title for the brochure. Check (✓) the correct answer.

_____ 1. Don't Drink Alcohol!

_____ 2. Beware! Drugs Are More Dangerous Than Alcohol!

_____ 3. The Facts about the Risks of Drugs and Alcohol

❷ **Finding Details** Match each of the following statements with the paragraph it is in.

___3___ Drugs can affect how you do in school.

_____ It can be dangerous to mix alcohol and drugs.

_____ Many people don't understand how dangerous drugs are.

_____ Drug abuse can break a family apart.

_____ Drugs can kill you.

_____ Hard drugs can destroy your brain.

_____ Diseases like AIDS can be spread by sharing needles.

_____ Drugs can affect how you think about your life.

❸ **Think about It** Work in a small group. Make a poster to persuade younger kids not to try tobacco, drugs or alcohol. Use the information in the brochure, as well as facts you already know

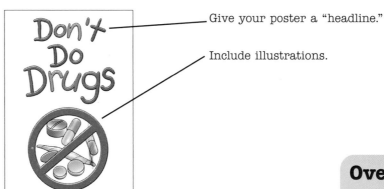

Give your poster a "headline."

Include illustrations.

❹ **Before You Move On** Put your posters on the wall. Take a "gallery walk." Rate each poster, then vote on the best poster.

Overall Rating

☆☆☆ I'm totally convinced!

☆☆ I'm pretty convinced.

☆ I'm not convinced.

D WORD WORK

1. Word Detective Match the word on the left with the correct definition on the right. What do you think the **boldfaced** parts of the words mean?

1. **non**smoker   a. to not like someone or something
2. **il**legal   b. not having many friends
3. **dis**like   c. not finished
4. **un**popular   d. against the law
5. **in**complete   e. someone who doesn't smoke cigarettes

2. Word Study Prefixes change the meaning of words. All of these common prefixes mean "not."

Prefix	Examples
non-	**non**drinker, **non**member, **non**sense
il-, in-, im-, ir-	**il**legal, **in**complete, **im**polite, **ir**regular
dis-	**dis**honest, **dis**loyal
un-	**un**believable, **un**important

3. Word Play Complete the sentences below. Use a prefix from the box below. You can use your dictionary.

il-	non-	dis-	in-	un-

SPELLING AND PHONICS: To do this activity, go to page 195.

1. It is _____*il*_ legal to sell drugs. If you're caught, you'll go to jail.
2. Sometimes I think my brother is crazy. I think he's _____sane!
3. My parents have _____skid tires on their car.
4. Maria's handwriting is _____legible. You can barely read what she writes!
5. I _____agree with many of your ideas. That's why we argue so often.
6. People who are _____kind usually don't have many friends.

E GRAMMAR   Gerunds as Subjects and Objects

1. Listen Up Listen to each sentence. Point your thumb up 👍 if it sounds correct. Point your thumb down 👎 if it sounds wrong.

👍 👎 1. Abuse drugs can be dangerous.

👍 👎 2. Stefan is unhappy about getting braces.

👍 👎 3. Quit cigarettes is hard for most people.

👍 👎 4. Paul's father quit smoke.

2. Learn the Rule Look at the chart below. After you have learned the rules, do Activity 1 again.

GERUNDS
1. A gerund is the *-ing* form of a verb used as a noun. Don't confuse it with the present progressive tense.
Gerund: ***Playing*** tennis is fun.   Present progressive: ***Is*** she ***playing*** tennis now?
2. A gerund can be the subject of a sentence.
Playing basketball is fun.   ***Smoking*** can make you feel dizzy.
3. A gerund can be the object of the verb.
Juan likes ***playing*** basketball.   Lori's father quit ***smoking*** last year.
4. A gerund can be the object of a preposition.
Tran is interested in ***playing*** basketball.   Our parents don't approve of ***smoking***.

3. Practice the Rule Each of the following sentences contains one or more errors. Cross out the error. Then rewrite each sentence correctly.

1. ~~Ride~~ with a drunk driver is dangerous.   *Riding with a drunk driver is dangerous.*
2. The boy enjoys play basketball.   _____
3. Drink and drive is illegal.   _____
4. Use drugs can damage your health.   _____
5. Try to quit drugs is usually difficult.   _____
6. My brother tried to stop smoke last year.   _____
7. Alice dislikes do her homework.   _____
8. Javier quit use drugs.   _____

| **F** | **BRIDGE TO WRITING** | Persuasive Writing |

1. Before You Read Talk with a partner. Why do you think some kids your age smoke? List three reasons.

2. Let's Read First, **skim** this "fact sheet" about smoking by reading each question. Then, as you read the answer to each question, write down facts you didn't know.

Each question states a common myth about smoking. Restate each myth in your own words.

THE REAL DEAL ABOUT TOBACCO

The Surgeon General says that 3,000 kids start smoking every day. They must not know the facts about tobacco. If they did, they'd stay miles away from the stuff! So let's cut through the smoke and get to the real deal about tobacco.

WE DON'T NEED TO WORRY—SMOKING WON'T AFFECT OUR HEALTH UNTIL WE'RE A LOT OLDER, RIGHT?

You already know that smoking can cause things like cancer and heart disease, but symptoms start to develop as soon as you smoke your first cigarette—no matter how young you are. These include shortness of breath, coughing, nausea, dizziness, and "phlegm production." Pretty gross, huh?

WELL, AT LEAST TOBACCO DOESN'T LEAD TO OTHER DRUG USE... DOES IT?

It doesn't always, but it certainly can. Many times tobacco is the first drug used by kids who use alcohol and illegal drugs. The Surgeon General says that, compared with nonsmokers, kids who smoke are three times more likely to use alcohol. They're eight times more likely to smoke marijuana, and 22 times more likely to use cocaine. Scary, huh?

The questions at the end of each paragraph make the writing friendly and personal.

WELL, IF SMOKING IS SO BAD, ALL YOU HAVE TO DO IS QUIT. HOW HARD CAN THAT BE?

Most teens who smoke want to stop. About 40 percent said they tried to quit and couldn't. Quitting is not a pretty sight because nicotine is as addictive as alcohol, heroin, or cocaine. The Surgeon General found that most smokers start before they finish high school. So if you make it to graduation day without starting to smoke, chances are you never will!

Source: "Surgeon General's Report for Kids about Smoking," published by U.S. Public Health Service

phlegm production—coughing up slimy mucus from the lungs

3. Making Content Connections Work with a partner to summarize the reading. What are some common ideas that people have about substances like drugs, alcohol, and tobacco that are false or untrue? What are the facts? Complete the chart below based on the readings and your own experiences.

For help with summarizing, complete Mini-Unit, Part C on page 190.

	Common misunderstandings	Facts
Drugs and alcohol		
Tobacco		

4. Expanding Your Vocabulary The words and phrases in the box describe some common effects of drugs and alcohol. Discuss the meanings of the words with a partner. Use the words to complete the chart below.

blurred vision	~~intoxication~~	bloodshot eyes	feeling dizzy
cancer	coughing	confusion	bad breath
lack of coordination	heart attack	nausea	suffocation

Drugs	Alcohol	Tobacco
	intoxication	

G WRITING CLINIC   Persuasive Writing

1. Think about It Which three kinds of writing often try to persuade others?

☐ recipe   ☐ brochure   ☐ poem

☐ poster   ☐ dictionary   ☐ bumper sticker

2. Focus on Organization

❶ Reread the first paragraph of the fact sheet for teens on smoking. What do you think the fact sheet will tell you? Check (✓) your answer.

_____   1. reasons why it is OK for kids to smoke

_____   2. reasons why it is not OK for kids to smoke

THE REAL DEAL ABOUT TOBACCO

The Surgeon General says that 3,000 kids start smoking every day. They must not know the facts about tobacco. If they did, they'd stay miles away from the stuff! So let's cut through the smoke and get to the real deal about tobacco.

The sentence in green is the opinion statement. This is the main point the writer will persuade you to believe.

❷ Reread the next two paragraphs.

WE DON'T NEED TO WORRY—SMOKING WON'T AFFECT OUR HEALTH UNTIL WE'RE A LOT OLDER, RIGHT?

You already know that smoking can cause things like cancer and heart disease, but symptoms start to develop as soon as you smoke your first cigarette—no matter how young you are. These include shortness of breath, coughing, nausea, dizziness, and "phlegm production." Pretty gross, huh?

WELL, AT LEAST TOBACCO DOESN'T LEAD TO OTHER DRUG USE... DOES IT?

It doesn't always, but it certainly can. Many times tobacco is the first drug used by kids who use alcohol and illegal drugs. The Surgeon General says that, compared with nonsmokers, kids who smoke are three times more likely to use alcohol. They're eight times more likely to smoke marijuana, and 22 times more likely to use cocaine. Scary, huh?

The words in yellow give reasons that kids should not smoke.

The words in blue provide facts and details to back up the reasons.

❸ Read more about smoking. Make a chart like this. Write the reasons kids should not smoke on the left side. Write facts, examples, and details on the right side. Use your own words.

Reasons Kids Shouldn't Smoke	Facts and Examples
Kids who smoke do not do as well in school as kids who do not.	

Kids who smoke think they're cool. Are they?

Only if by "cool" you mean kids who probably aren't doing very well in school. The Surgeon General found that students with the highest grades are less likely to smoke than those with the lowest grades. Tobacco use is highest among drop-outs, lowest among college students.

Kids who smoke have lower self-images. They look to smoking because they think it will give them a better image—cooler, maybe, or more attractive, or more popular. And because their self-image is low, they don't have the confidence to say no when someone wants them to use tobacco.

drop-out—a kid who leaves school

self-image—how you see yourself

look to—to turn your attention to

3. Focus on Style Brochures often use subheadings to help organize the information. When you are writing to persuade other people, questions can be a good way to highlight each main point you want to make. Match the questions on the left to the correct main point on the right.

1. Is it harmful to smoke when you're young?
2. Does tobacco use lead to other drugs?
3. Is it hard to quit?

a. Because smoking is addictive, it is very difficult to stop.
b. Smoking at any age is harmful.
c. Tobacco is often the first drug used by kids who later use alcohol and illegal drugs.

H WRITER'S WORKSHOP   Persuasive Writing

Write a brochure for teens on drugs or alcohol. It should convince other teens that drug and alcohol use is dangerous and foolish.

1. Getting It Out

❶ Begin by learning the facts.

Facts about Alcohol

✓ Affects your brain (loss of coordination, slow movement, confusion, fuzzy vision, blackouts).

✓ Affects your body (damages organs, can cause cancer).

✓ Affects self-control (you don't behave like yourself, can lead to risky behaviors).

✓ Can kill you (causes many teen traffic deaths, too much can lead to coma or even death).

✓ More dangerous for teens to drink than adults (harms growing bodies and minds, teens who drink are more likely to become alcoholics later).

✓ It is illegal to buy or carry alcohol if you are under 21.

Facts about Inhalants

✓ Affect your brain (cause an instant high, can destroy your brain before you know it).

✓ Affect your heart (force the heart to beat out of control, starve the body of oxygen).

✓ Damage other parts of the body (cause you to vomit, cause nosebleeds, destroy muscles).

✓ Can cause sudden death the first time you use them (from choking, heart attacks, suffocation).

Facts about Marijuana

✓ Many teens believe it's not harmful, but it is.

✓ Affects your brain (makes it hard to remember, can make you "see things," makes it hard to think, makes it hard to do things like drive, play sports, or read).

✓ Affects your body (makes your heart beat fast, can cause lung cancer).

✓ Affects your attitude (can make you not care about things, can make it hard for you to learn).

✓ Illegal in every state (you could go to jail).

✓ Most kids who use hard drugs (like cocaine or heroin) begin by using marijuana.

✓ Hard for many people to quit.

---

self-control—the ability to control what you say and do   oxygen—the air you breathe to stay alive

inhalant—a drug you inhale, often fumes from products like glue or paint thinner

❷ Choose the topic of your brochure. Copy and complete the chart below to help you organize your ideas.

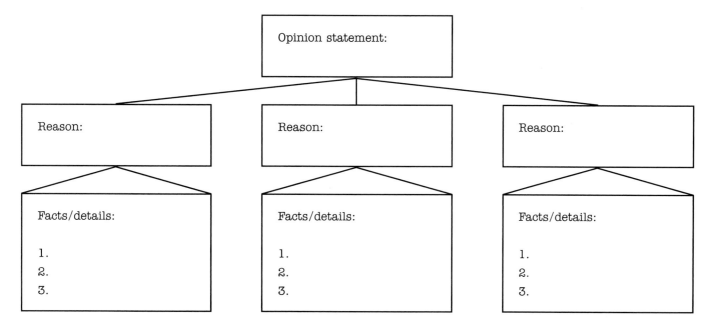

Opinion statement:

Reason: | Reason: | Reason:

Facts/details:

1.
2.
3.

Facts/details:

1.
2.
3.

Facts/details:

1.
2.
3.

❸ Here is Juan's chart.

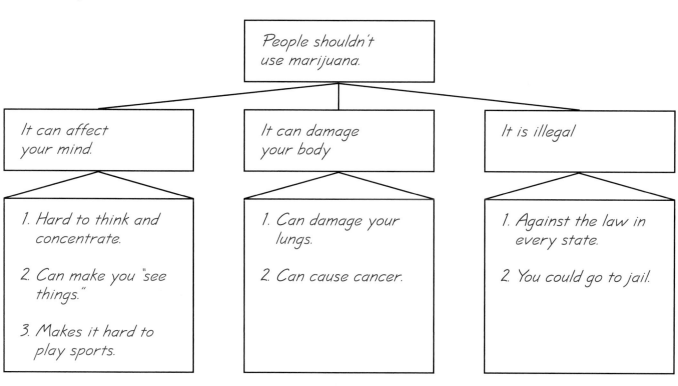

People shouldn't use marijuana.

It can affect your mind. | It can damage your body | It is illegal

1. Hard to think and concentrate.

2. Can make you "see things."

3. Makes it hard to play sports.

1. Can damage your lungs.

2. Can cause cancer.

1. Against the law in every state.

2. You could go to jail.

2. Getting It Down

❶ Use your diagram to make an outline for your brochure.

Title: _____

Opinion statement: _____ .

1. Reason: _____ .

   a. Fact/example/detail: _____ .

   b. Fact/example/detail: _____ .

2. Reason: _____ .

   a. Fact/example/detail: _____ .

   b. Fact/example/detail: _____ .

─ MINI-LESSON ─

Using Dashes:
Use a dash (—) in a sentence when you want the reader to notice information:

Eat healthy foods—fruit, vegetables, and fish.

❷ Turn your outline into several short paragraphs. Here is what Juan wrote:

Marijuana Madness

Many teens think that marijuana is not harmful. They couldn't be more wrong! Using marijuana is foolish, and it can be dangerous.

Marijuana can affect your brain. It can make it hard to think clearly and to concentrate on what you're doing. That means you're unable to do things that require concentration—fun things like driving a car, shooting hoops, or reading a really good book. It can even make you think you're seeing things that aren't there!

Marijuana can also harm your body. It can weaken your body and make it harder to fight diseases. It can damage your lungs and even cause lung cancer.

That's probably why marijuana is illegal in all 50 states. Is it really worth going to jail just for a marijuana cigarette?

❸ Look at what Juan wrote. Did he leave anything out that would make his brochure even better? Use the following chart to check.

_____ 1. Has a title.

_____ 2. Has an opinion statement.

_____ 3. Uses subheadings.

_____ 4. Gives at least two reasons.

_____ 5. Provides facts and details.

_____ 6. Has a strong conclusion.

3. Getting It Right Take a careful look at what you have written. Use these questions to help you review and revise your work.

Questions to ask . . .	How to check . . .	How to revise . . .
1. Does my introduction state my opinion?	Ask a neighbor to find the opinion statement in your introduction.	Add a sentence that clearly states your opinion.
2. Do I use subheadings with questions to help organize the information?	Put a star (★) in front of each subheading.	Add subheadings. Use short phrases or questions.
3. Do I give at least two reasons to support my opinion?	<u>Underline</u> each reason.	Add one or more reasons.
4. Do I provide facts and details to support each reason?	Circle each fact or detail.	Add facts to support your reasons.

4. Presenting It Read your brochure to your classmates. Take notes on a chart like the one below as you listen to other students. Give each student's presentation an overall rating.

Reasons	Facts and Details

Overall Rating

☆☆☆ Very convincing
☆☆   Convincing
☆   Not convincing

1. On Assignment Imagine that it is Drug Prevention Week at your school. Your class has to write and act in an anti-drug skit (a short play). Work in groups of four or five.

❶ Decide on the characters, a problem, and a place for the action.

❷ Brainstorm your story. Make a story timeline.

☐ Think about the opening part. How will you first tell the audience about the main problem?

☐ Think about the middle. How will the main characters try to solve the problem?

☐ Think about the ending. How will everything end?

❸ Now write a script. Write the words that each character will say. Make your characters sound like they are really talking naturally.

> *Donna: Here...have a cigarette! Smoking is cool!*
> *Juan: Are you crazy? Smoking is very uncool!*

❹ Edit your script.

☐ What is the message you want others to get from your skit? Is your message clear?

☐ Will your skit convince the audience?

☐ Do your characters and the dialog (the words your characters say) like people really talk?

❺ Perform your skit.

2. Link to Literature

🎧 **SHARED READING** *Go Ask Alice* is the true story of a teenager's slide into the world of drugs. It is based on the actual diary of a fifteen-year-old drug user. Read two entries from Alice's diary.

April 6

... I'm really going to try to make kids see that getting into drugs simply isn't worth [it]. Sure, it's great and groovy going on trips, I will never be able to say it isn't. It's exciting and colorful and dangerous, but it isn't worth it! It simply isn't worth it! Every day for the rest of my life I shall dread weakening again and becoming something I simply do not want to be! I'll have to fight it every day of my life ...

April 19

Cripes! It's started again! I met Jan downtown and she asked me to a "party" tonight. None of the kids think I'm going to really stay off, because most of those who have been busted before are just being more careful and discreet. When I told Jan, "No, thanks," she just smiled. It scared me to death. She didn't say anything at all. She just smiled at me like, "We know you'll be back." I hope not. Oh, I really hope not.

Source: *Go Ask Alice*

groovy—a word used in the 1960s meaning "cool"

trip—an experience someone has when taking an illegal drug

discreet—careful not to tell information that you want to keep secret

LET'S TALK

1. How does Alice feel about drugs?
2. How hard is it for kids to get off of drugs, once they have started?
3. Who is probably right—Alice or her friend Jan?
4. Talk with a partner. Which is more persuasive—a brochure about drugs or a real-life story like *Go Ask Alice*?

Unit 9

I Love Jell-O®!

Read…

■ A review of one guy's favorite fizzy treat.

■ An explanation of why a gooey breakfast can be delicious.

Link to Literature

■ A review of the book *Falling Up*, by Shel Silverstein and "Tattooin' Ruth," a poem from that book.

Objectives:

Reading:

■ Evaluation: Reading food reviews
■ Strategies: Visualizing and summarizing
■ Literature: Reading a book review

Writing:

■ Evaluation: Writing reviews
■ Justifying an opinion
■ Using stand-out adjectives

Vocabulary:

■ Recognizing antonyms
■ Using descriptive adjectives

Listening/Speaking:

■ Listening to descriptions
■ Comparing two things
■ Stating and justifying an opinion

Grammar:

■ Using adverbial clauses of condition (*if* clauses)

Spelling and Phonics:

■ Spelling the /j/ sound as in *jam* and *badge*

Sparkling Grape Jell-O®

BEFORE YOU BEGIN

Talk with your classmates.

1. Look at the picture. What do you see? Help your teacher make a list.

2. Read the caption. What is the name of the product?

3. Have you ever eaten Jell-O®? What is it like? If not, what do you think it would be like from the picture?

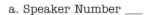

| A | CONNECTING TO YOUR LIFE |

 **1. Tuning In** Listen to the descriptions. Match the speakers with the pictures.

a. Speaker Number ___

b. Speaker Number ___

c. Speaker Number ___

d. Speaker Number ___

e. Speaker Number ___

f. Speaker Number _1_

2. Talking It Over On the chart below, write the name of a food you eat in the school cafeteria. Rate the food by circling a number for each question.

Find a classmate who rated the same food. Compare your ratings.

Name of food:	Rating				
_____	Excellent	Very good	Good	Fair	Poor
1. How does it look?	4	3	2	1	0
2. How does it taste?	4	3	2	1	0
3. How does it smell?	4	3	2	1	0
5. How much does it cost?	4	3	2	1	0
6. Is it good for you?	4	3	2	1	0

Read the title of this unit. What do you think this unit is probably about? Check (✓) the correct answer.

_____ 1. foods that begin with "J"

_____ 2. foods that people love

_____ 3. foods that can make you ill

B GETTING READY TO READ

1. Learning New Words Read the sentences below. Try to guess the meanings of the underlined words.

1. I am completely sure that you will like the restaurant. I <u>guarantee</u> you will love the food.
2. This apple tastes so sweet and juicy! It's <u>delicious</u>.
3. Eating fruit has many <u>benefits</u>! It tastes good, it fills you up, and it's good for you.
4. Juan loves all cookies, but chocolate chip and peanut butter cookies are his <u>favorites</u>.
5. There are many <u>varieties</u> of pizza on the menu: mushroom, pepperoni, four-cheese, and deluxe.
6. The food in the cafeteria gives your body lots of good things. It is <u>nutritious</u>.

Now match each word on the left with the correct definition on the right.

1. nutritious   a. tasting good
2. guarantee   b. a positive result
3. favorite   c. having things that keep you healthy
4. delicious   d. something someone likes best
5. benefit   e. to promise
6. varieties   f. different types

2. Talking It Over Work in groups of three or four.

❶ List ten foods you all eat. Complete the chart below. Put each food in the correct column. Which column has the longest list? Why?

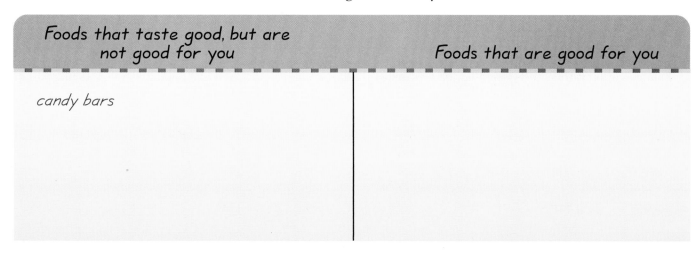

Foods that taste good, but are not good for you	Foods that are good for you
candy bars	

❷ Choose one of the foods. Make a poster that makes others want to eat it.

C READING TO LEARN

1. Before You Read Do you remember a time when you thought you wouldn't like something, but you loved it when you ate it? Share this experience with a partner.

2. Let's Read Read the following selection. It is a review of a common dessert, Jell-O®. As you read, **visualize** what it would be like to eat Sparking Grape Jell-O® for the first time.

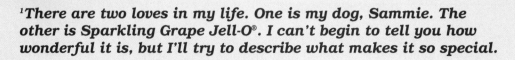 by Casey D.

> This is an effective opening. Casey's words make you want to keep reading.

¹*There are two loves in my life. One is my dog, Sammie. The other is Sparkling Grape Jell-O®. I can't begin to tell you how wonderful it is, but I'll try to describe what makes it so special.*

² The first time I tried Sparkling Grape Jell-O®, I was sick with strep throat and had to stay home from school. My mom went to the store and brought back a pint of Ben and Jerry's and two packets of Jell-O®, one cherry, which is boring, and Sparkling Grape. Normally, I hate Jell-O®, but my mom made the Sparkling Grape with carbonated water. Several hours later, she put a bowl in front of me. Cautiously, I took a tiny spoonful and the amazing taste of Concord grapes with an explosion of bubbles went down my throat. From then on I was hooked. Now, I eat Sparkling Grape Jell-O® as often as possible. I still haven't gotten tired of that cool, tingly feeling every time I put a spoonful in my mouth.

³ I guarantee a great meal if you add Sparkling Grape Jell-O® to your menu. It is refreshing, exciting, and delicious!

> Casey's closing paragraph makes you want to try Sparkling Grape Jell-O!

Source: teenink.com

strep throat—an illness that causes a very sore throat

Ben and Jerry's—a popular brand of ice cream

normally—usually

carbonated—liquid having many tiny bubbles

cautiously—very carefully, to avoid danger

Concord—a type of sweet, purple grape

explosion—a sudden burst

hooked—liking something a lot

tingly—slightly stinging

refreshing—making someone feel pleasant and less tired or hot

3. Unlocking Meaning

❶ **Finding the Main Idea** Casey wrote his review mostly because he wants to do what? Check (✓) the correct answer.

_____ 1. compare Sparkling Grape Jell-O® to cherry Jell-O®

_____ 2. explain how to make Sparkling Grape Jell-O®

_____ 3. convince other people to try Sparkling Grape Jell-O®

❷ **Finding Details** Reread the selection on Jell-O®. Which of the following reasons does Casey give for loving Sparkling Grape Jell-O®? Check (✓) the correct answers.

_____ 1. His dog Sammie loves it.

_____ 2. It is delicious.

_____ 3. It is purple instead of red, like cherry.

_____ 4. It feels good when you eat it.

_____ 5. You can eat it with a spoon.

_____ 6. The bubbles give it a tingly feeling.

_____ 7. It is made from grapes, his favorite fruit.

❸ **Think about It** Work in groups of three or four.

1. Decide on three foods that everyone in the group likes a lot.
2. List at least four reasons that you like each food. Complete the chart below.
3. Share your chart with your classmates. Did other groups describe the same foods?

Food #1	Food #2	Food #3
_____	_____	_____

❹ **Before You Move On** Give Casey's review a more interesting title— one that would make you really want to read the review.

D WORD WORK

1. Word Detective Match each word on the left with the word on the right that means the opposite or almost the opposite.

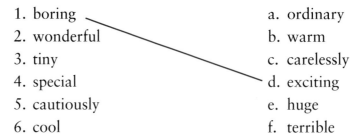

1. boring	a. ordinary
2. wonderful	b. warm
3. tiny	c. carelessly
4. special	d. exciting
5. cautiously	e. huge
6. cool	f. terrible

boring

2. Word Study An antonym is a word with a meaning opposite (or almost opposite) that of another word. Do the Word Detective activity again, using your dictionary. Look at the following examples of antonyms.

a. Plain crackers are <u>boring</u>. Sparkling Grape Jell-O® is <u>exciting</u>.
b. Pizza is served <u>hot</u>. Jell-O® is served <u>cold</u>.

exciting

3. Word Play Work with a partner. Think of the opposite of each word or phrase in the chart below. Write pairs of sentences using both words. You can use your dictionary.

1. sweet	2. good for you	3. expensive	4. soft
sour			
5. frozen	6. thick (crust)	7. delicious	8. best

1. <u>*Ice cream is sweet. Lemons are sour.*</u>
2. _____
3. _____
4. _____
5. _____
6. _____
7. _____
8. _____

SPELLING AND PHONICS:
To do this activity, go to page 196.

E GRAMMAR *If* Clauses

1. Listen Up Listen to each sentence. Point your thumb up 👍 if it sounds correct. Point your thumb down 👎 if it sounds wrong.

👍 👎 1. If it will rain tomorrow, you will need an umbrella.

👍 👎 2. If the doorbell rings, I will answer the door.

👍 👎 3. If Rosa will win the race, she will win a prize.

👍 👎 4. If you work hard, you will be successful.

2. Learn the Rule Learn how to express what will happen if something else happens. Then do Activity 1 again.

ADVERBIAL CLAUSES OF CONDITION (*IF* CLAUSES)
1. An *if* clause in a sentence talks about something that may or may not happen (a possible condition). The main clause identifies a possible **result**.
If you are late for school, you will get detention.
2. Use the present tense in an *if* clause, even though the clause refers to a time in the future.
Right: If I **am** still sick tomorrow, I **will** stay home from school.   Wrong: If I ~~will~~ still ~~be~~ sick tomorrow, I will stay home from school.

3. Practice the Rule Work with a partner. Match each condition with the correct result.

CONDITION

1. If Juan wins the tennis tournament,
2. If Juan misses the bus,
3. If Juan wins the lottery,
4. If Juan eats too many sweets,
5. If Juan gets straight A's,
6. If Juan's parents give him permission,
7. If Juan doesn't do his chores,

RESULT

a. his teeth will fall out.
b. he won't get his allowance.
c. he will sleep over at Matt's house.
d. he will be late to school.
e. he will take home a trophy.
f. he will be named "Student of the Month."
g. he will buy his parents a new house.

F BRIDGE TO WRITING   Evaluation

For help with summarizing, complete Mini-Unit, Part C on page 190.

1. Before You Read Write down your favorite breakfast food. Compare your answer with your classmates.

🎧 **2. Let's Read** Read about oatmeal, a popular hot cereal. After each paragraph, **summarize** what Keith says.

READING STRATEGY

Summarizing:
When you summarize, you restate the main points in an article, using your own words. This lets you see if you've really understood.
■■■

Keith writes like he is talking to you. Why does he do this?

Oatmeal

by Keith P.

¹ **Oatmeal.** Usually people think of a mushy bowl of goo. I, however, think it is a great way to start the day. Every morning have a nice, warm breakfast to wake you up. You can eat oatmeal fast, too, which is handy if you overslept and must make a mad dash for the bus.

² **Oatmeal** is very tasty and comes in many varieties. My favorites are "Maple and Brown Sugar" and "Cinnamon and Spice." There are other flavors if you don't particularly enjoy these two.

³ **Oatmeal** tastes good when you add stuff to it, too. I like raisins and walnuts. It is filling; a bowl in the morning should keep you from getting hungry until lunch.

⁴ Another benefit of eating oatmeal is that it's actually nutritious! Instead of having a bowl of sugary cereal that's not good for you and will rot your teeth, you can eat oatmeal. Studies show that oatmeal reduces cholesterol and the risk of heart attacks. It's also a good source of calcium, fiber, iron and other vitamins and minerals.

⁵ **Oatmeal** is an excellent way to start your day every morning. I highly suggest you try it.

⁶ **Yum.**

Source: teenink.com

goo—a thick and sticky substance

make a mad dash—to hurry

flavor—the taste of food or drink

reduce—to make smaller or less in number or amount

cholesterol—a substance in your blood that can cause heart disease

source—where something comes from

fiber—a substance in vegetables, fruits, and grains that help move food through your body

vitamin—a substance in foods that helps you grow and stay healthy

mineral—a substance that humans, animals, and plants need to grow. **Calcium** and **iron** are minerals.

yum—you say this when something tastes good.

3. Making Content Connections You have read two food reviews. Now, work with a partner. Compare the reviews. Complete the chart below.

	Casey's Review	**Keith's Review**
1. What reasons does the author give for liking the food?	*It is fun to eat because it has bubbles in it.*	
2. In your opinion, what is the best reason the author gives for eating the food?		
3. Based on the review, would you try the food? Why or why not?		

4. Expanding Your Vocabulary Work in groups of three or four. Think of a food you all love. Complete the chart below. Use the words and phrases in the box, or use different words. You can use your dictionary to find different words.

Some words might go in more than one place in the chart.

salty	crispy	golden	crunchy
covered with	bubbling hot	full of	satisfied
frosty	chewy	sweet	delicious
enormous	sour	content	spicy

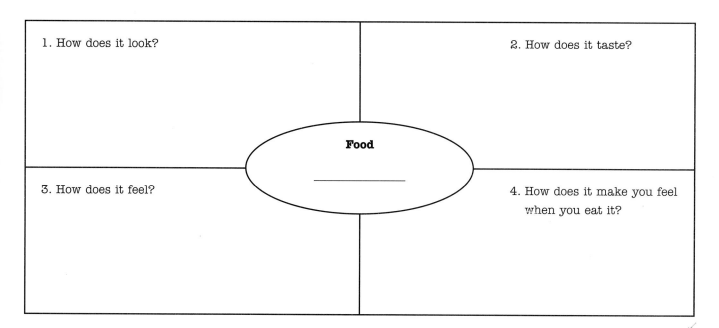

1. How does it look?

2. How does it taste?

Food

_____

3. How does it feel?

4. How does it make you feel when you eat it?

| G | WRITING CLINIC | Evaluation |

1. Think about It Where can you probably find reviews like you just read? In a—

☐ textbook.   ☐ magazine or newspaper   ☐ book of recipes   ☐ collection of short stories

2. Focus on Organization

❶ Take another look at Keith's review of oatmeal.

> Keith begins his review by telling you his **opinion** about oatmeal.

> He gives **reasons** for liking oatmeal.

> He **describes** oatmeal.

> He writes as if he is talking to the reader. The words "I" and "you" give his review a voice.

> He gives **details** and **facts** to back up his reasons.

> He ends his review by urging the reader to try oatmeal.

> Why is this line such a good way to end the review?

Oatmeal

¹ **Oatmeal.** Usually people think of a mushy bowl of goo. I, however, think it is a great way to start the day. Every morning have a nice, warm breakfast to wake you up. You can eat oatmeal fast, too, which is handy if you pulled the "five more minutes" move or just overslept and must make a mad dash for the bus.

² **Oatmeal** is very tasty and comes in many varieties. My favorites are "Maple and Brown Sugar" and "Cinnamon and Spice." There are other flavors if you don't particularly enjoy these two.

³ **Oatmeal** tastes good when you add stuff to it, too. I like raisins and walnuts. It is filling; a bowl in the morning should keep you from getting hungry until lunch.

⁴ Another benefit of eating oatmeal is that it's actually nutritious! Instead of having a bowl of sugary cereal that's not good for you and will rot your teeth, you can eat oatmeal. Studies show that oatmeal reduces cholesterol and the risk of heart attacks. It's also a good source of calcium, fiber, iron and other vitamins and minerals.

⁵ **Oatmeal** is an excellent way to start your day every morning. I highly suggest you try it.

⁶ **Yum.**

❷ Good reviews give lots of reasons, details, and facts. Find the reasons, details, and facts that Keith gives for eating oatmeal. Complete the chart below.

Qualities/Characteristics	Reasons	Details/Facts
1. convenience	You can eat oatmeal fast.	This is handy if you overslept.
2. taste		
3. satisfaction		
4. health benefits		

3. Focus on Style

❶ Reviews often use stand-out adjectives to describe.

1. Usually people think of a mushy bowl of goo.
2. It's handy if you have to make a mad dash for the bus.

❷ Imagine the perfect slice of pizza. Match the adjectives to the traits below.

TRAITS

___c___ 1. how it looks (appearance)

_____ 4. how much it costs (price)

_____ 2. how it tastes (taste)

_____ 5. how it fills you up (satisfaction)

_____ 3. how it feels to eat (texture)

ADJECTIVES

a. filling
b. chewy
c. crusty
d. spicy
e. inexpensive

H WRITER'S WORKSHOP   Evaluation

Imagine that you have been invited to write a review for the food section of your local newspaper.

1. Getting It Out

❶ Choose a food to review. Select something that—

☐ you really love to eat and eat often
☐ other people might not know about or have tried yet
☐ will be fun for others to read about

Here are some ideas.

1.

A burrito

2.

Granola bars and breakfast bars

3.

Egg rolls

4.

Papayas

❷ Describe the food. Use a diagram like this. On your own, brainstorm what the food is like.

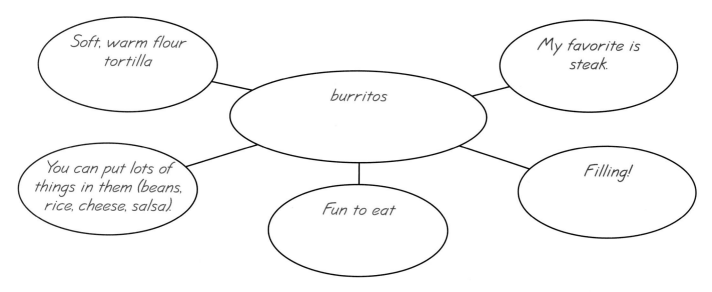

❸ Now decide which traits you will discuss. Think about your reasons then add details. Complete the chart below.

Traits	Reasons	Details/Facts
1. *taste*	*delicious*	
2. *appearance*		
3.		
4.		

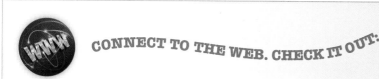

CONNECT TO THE WEB. CHECK IT OUT:

Read the reviews that other teens have written at www.teenink.com

2. Getting It Down

❶ Make an outline like this.

<u>Opinion statement:</u> *One of my favorite foods is...* .

1. <u>Reason:</u> *It's easy to fix.* .

   <u>Detail/Fact:</u> *Ready in just five minutes* .

2. <u>Reason:</u> .

   <u>Detail/Fact:</u> .

3. <u>Reason:</u> .

   <u>Detail/Fact:</u> .

   <u>Conclusion:</u> .

The review has an **opinion statement.**

Sau-Lim **describes** the food.

Sau-Lim provides **reasons and details.**

Sau-Lim uses **stand-out adjectives.**

❷ Draft your review using your outline to help you. Here is what Sau-Lim wrote.

Couscous

One of my favorite foods is something you may never have tried—couscous. You'll find it on the table in any North African home. It's made from tiny grains of semolina (wheat). You can eat it by itself, in a stew, or with meat and vegetables.

Couscous is rapidly growing in popularity in the U.S. There are many good reasons! It's quick and easy to cook. Just add water, and five minutes later, it's ready to eat!

It's also delicious. I love to add spices and onions and top it with cheese. I love the nutty taste and zesty aroma!

Finally, it's good for you. Couscous contains only 100 to 120 calories per half-cup serving, and it is loaded with vitamins and minerals.

Even if you have never heard of couscous, you should give it a try. You'll soon be hooked on couscous!

— MINI-LESSON —

Using Commas:
Use a comma after adverbs that begin a sentence:

Finally, it's good for you.

3. Getting It Right Look carefully at your review. Use this guide to revise your paragraph.

Ask yourself...	How to check...	How to revise...
1. Does my review have an opinion statement?	<u>Underline</u> your opinion statement.	Tell the reader exactly how you feel about the food or product.
2. Do I describe the food or product?	Show your draft to a neighbor. Ask them to describe the food in their own words.	Change your description so that others will know more about the food.
3. Do I give reasons for my opinion?	<u>Draw a wavy line</u> under each reason.	Provide more than one reason.
4. Do I give details to back up each reason?	Put a check mark (✓) next to each detail.	Add details that will convince your reader.
5. Do I use stand-out adjectives?	Circle each adjective.	Add an adjective or two to make your review interesting.

4. Presenting It Share the page you have written with your classmates.

❶ Read your first paragraph aloud. Make sure that your classmates know how you feel about the food.

❷ Read the rest of your review aloud. Read slowly and speak clearly.

❸ Ask for feedback from your classmates.

I never heard of couscous before. Now I know what it is.

You gave a lot of reasons—not just one or two!

Your review made me hungry! I want to try couscous.

1. On Assignment

❶ Work in groups of three or four. Read newspaper reviews.

1. Choose one of the following reviews to read.
2. Make a list of the words nobody in your group knows. Try to guess the meaning. Use a dictionary to check your guesses.
3. Choose someone in your group to read the review aloud. Think about how you will teach your classmates the new words.
4. Which review is the most fun to read? Why?

NOW PLAYING

BAD BOYS VIII

In the silliest of plots, Miami cops try to bring down a ring of mobsters. Once again, Will Smith and Martin Lawrence play trash-talking detectives. It's hard to tell the good guys from the bad boys. (R: strong violence and action, language, and crude humor). D2

DINING OUT

Pizzeria Uno

Great pizza and surroundings that make you think you're in Italy. The menu offers a wide variety for all. Takeout is available. Two convenient locations. Highly recommended. A+

VIDEO GAMES

NFL2K1

Incredible graphics, awesome control system, and great fun factor. You'll be wondering if you are playing or watching Monday Night Football. The greatest football game ever made! A

HIP-HOP/R&B

WHAT: Housebroken

WHO: Woof Woof Dawg

GRADE: F

Woof Woof's second album makes you want to give the teen rapper up for adoption. Thirteen tracks with dumb lyrics that will make you bare your teeth. Spend your money on dog biscuits instead.

❷ Write your own short review.

1. Choose something to review.
2. Give it an overall grade, from A+ to F.
3. Decide why you gave it that grade. Make a list of reasons.
4. Write a review with three or four sentences.
5. Share with your classmates.

🎧 **SHARED READING** Reviews can also be about literature. Read Amy P.'s review of *Falling Up*.

Falling Up
by Shel Silverstein
Review by Amy P.

For me, poetry is a very personal thing. It makes me laugh, and sometimes even cry. I love poetry for what it says about life, about love, and about everything in this world that is worth writing about. When I think of great poetry, *Falling Up* by Shel Silverstein comes to mind. Its humorous poems are always what I need for a good laugh, and they help lighten my mood.

This is a collection of the silliest and zaniest poems you can imagine. They are hilarious, and good for readers of all ages. I have been reading Silverstein's poems since I was little, and I loved them even then. Some are extremely clever, like "The Monkey," and others are just plain funny, like "Tattooin' Ruth".

I highly recommend this book to anyone who appreciates poetry and likes to laugh. I guarantee you'll enjoy it. The book's wacky nature will make anyone crack a smile, and you can be sure that you'll be flipping through the pages for a long time to come!

LET'S TALK Answer the questions.

Source: teenink.com

1. What reasons does Amy give for liking the book?
2. Read the poem "Tattooin' Ruth." Do you agree with Amy?
3. Does the review make you want to read the book? Why or why not?

ABOUT THE AUTHOR

Shel Silverstein was born in Chicago, Illinois in 1930 and died in 1999. He wrote many fun stories and poems. Some of his most famous books are *The Giving Tree*, *Where the Sidewalk Ends*, and *Falling Up*.

TATTOOIN' RUTH

Collars are choking,
Pants are expensive,
Jackets are itchy and hot,
So tattooin' Ruth tattooed me a suit.
Now folks think I'm *dressed*—
When I'm not.

Source: *Falling Up* by Shel Silverstein

humorous—funny

zany—funny in an unusual way

hilarious—very, very funny

clever—original

wacky—very silly

crack a smile—to begin to smile

Unit 10

Let's Debate!

Read...

- An article about a law that could force students to be polite.

- An article about taking junk food out of school cafeterias.

Link to Literature

- "How to Successfully Persuade Your Parents to Give You More Pocket Money," a poem by Andrea Shavick.

Objectives:

Reading:
- Evaluating feature articles that present two sides of an issue
- Strategies: Identifying facts and opinions, skimming for information
- Literature: Responding to a poem

Writing:
- Writing a feature article: A debate
- Writing an introduction that provides background information
- Using facts and quotes both to interest and convince others

Vocabulary:
- Recognizing word families
- Learning words and phrases used in discussion and debate

Listening/Speaking:
- Listening to the discussion of an issue
- Stating an opinion
- Presenting arguments to support your opinion

Grammar:
- Using modals to help persuade others

Sounds and Spelling:
- Spelling the /or/ sound as in *for* and *four*

For and against

BEFORE YOU BEGIN

Talk with your classmates.

1. Look at the picture. What do you think is happening?
2. Read the words on the blackboard. What is the girl probably telling her classmates?
3. Do kids have too much homework? Should they have more?

A CONNECTING TO YOUR LIFE

1. Tuning In Listen to the conversation between Erik and his mother. Whose side do you take? Why?

2. Talking It Over Read the survey. Circle an answer for each question?

	YES	NO
1. Should kids have to take gym?	☺	☹
2. Should kids give themselves their own grades?	☺	☹
3. Should there be separate schools for girls and boys?	☺	☹

Find out what your classmates think. Choose one question from the survey that interests you. Ask five other people what they think.

Question: _____

Write one reason for each person's answer.

EXAMPLE:

Person 1: Answer: __yes__   Reason: _Kids need exercise for good health._

Person 2: Answer: _____   Reason: _____

Person 3: Answer: _____   Reason: _____

Person 4: Answer: _____   Reason: _____

Person 5: Answer: _____   Reason: _____

Read the title. What do you think the unit is probably about? Check (✓) the correct answer.

_____ 1. topics or questions most people agree on

_____ 2. topics or questions people often disagree about

_____ 3. topics or questions that are silly

B GETTING READY TO READ

1. Learning New Words Read the sentences below. Try to guess the meanings of the underlined words.

1. If you steal, you may go to jail because stealing is against the <u>law</u>.
2. Lori bumped into Sarah. She didn't even have the <u>courtesy</u> to apologize!
3. Students must take gym. It's <u>required</u>.
4. There are three good <u>arguments</u> for not cheating. First, it's wrong. Second, it's against school rules. Third, you won't learn anything.
5. We shouldn't allow skateboards at school. We should <u>ban</u> them!
6. Children can't decide if they want to go to school or stay home. They have no <u>choice</u>.
7. Juan thinks wearing bicycle helmets is a good idea because helmets save lives. That is his <u>position</u>.

Now match each word on the left with the correct definition on the right.

1. law   a. necessary because of a law or rule
2. courtesy   b. an opinion about something
3. required   c. a rule in a country, state, or city that we must follow
4. argument   d. the right to choose something
5. ban   e. polite behavior to other people
6. choice   f. an explanation you give for what you believe
7. position   g. to order that an activity must not happen

2. Talking It Over Work in groups of three or four. List three laws that you know about. Discuss why we need each law. Complete the chart below.

Laws	Why we need these laws
EXAMPLE: *It's against the law to break the speed limit.*	*Driving too fast causes accidents.*
1.	
2.	
3.	

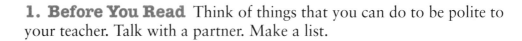

---READING STRATEGY---
Identifying Facts and Opinions:
Identifying facts and opinions can help you evaluate, or analyze, an argument or point of view. ■ ■ ■

1. Before You Read Think of things that you can do to be polite to your teacher. Talk with a partner. Make a list.

2. Let's Read Read the article. It discusses two sides of a question that people have strong feelings about. As you read, **identify the facts and opinions.** Then decide with side you agree with most.

Do Students Need a Courtesy Law? (Debate)

[1] In Louisiana's public schools, being polite to teachers isn't just expected—it's required by state law. In 1999, Louisiana passed the first student respect law. It requires students to address their teachers as "sir" or "ma'am," or with appropriate titles, such as "Mrs." or "Mr."

[2] "Just as we teach reading and writing, I think we can teach manners," says Donald Cravins, the state senator who sponsored the law.

[3] The idea has spread quickly. Several other states are considering similar laws. But not everyone agrees that courtesy laws are a good idea. What do you think? Should students be required by law to be polite? Read both arguments, then decide.

Yes, Ma'am!

[4] Teachers don't get enough respect from students today. Courtesy laws will help students and teachers work together to create an environment that fosters creativity and learning.

[5] With courtesy laws in effect, teachers can spend less time disciplining their students and more time teaching them. "I've had teacher after teacher tell me that it's changed the whole experience in the classroom," says Louisiana Governor Mike Foster.

[6] Many students agree that some kids need to learn better manners. "I think a courtesy law would help some kids show respect at home," says Kurt Phelan.

Yes, sir.

Louisiana

The arguments "for" always come first.

expected—considered to be the thing that people should do

respect—being polite to someone because they are important

manners—polite ways of behaving

senator—a member of the Senate, one of two groups that makes laws

sponsor—to push for (a new law)

consider—to think about doing something

environment—the situation or people that affect how you live, learn, or work

foster—help something happen

creativity—using your imagination to do things

discipline—to punish for bad behavior

No, Sir!

7   Good manners should be taught at home by parents, not in the schools. "Teachers deserve respect because they are adults," says 17-year old Peter Lainey. "But that decision should be left up to the parents."

8   These kinds of laws only take attention away from the real problems that plague schools today. School districts need to build better schools, reduce drop-out rates, improve test scores, and raise teachers' salaries to really improve education.

9   "'Yes, ma'am' and 'no, ma'am' is fine, says Sue Hall, a teacher in New Orleans. "But it's pretty superficial. You're not getting to the root of the problem."

Source: *Junior Scholastic*

plague—to cause trouble again and again

reduce—to make smaller or less in number or amount

drop-out rates—the numbers of kids quitting school

improve—to make better

superficial—not very important

root—the main or basic part

❶ **Finding the Main Idea** What is the main idea of this article? Check (✓) the correct answer.

_____   1. Most people favor courtesy laws.

_____   2. Some people favor courtesy laws and others do not.

_____   3. Most states will soon pass a courtesy law.

❷ **Finding Details** Listen as your teacher reads each of the statements. Point your thumb up 👍 if it is an argument **for** courtesy laws. Point your thumb down 👎 if it is an argument **against** such laws.

👍👎 1. Courtesy laws will make students show more respect for their teachers.

👍👎 2. Schools have more important problems to deal with than teaching manners.

👍👎 3. Courtesy laws help students learn better.

👍👎 4. Good manners should be taught at home, not school.

👍👎 5. Teachers will have fewer discipline problems.

❸ **Think about It** Work with a partner. Think of one more argument for each position. Write down your arguments and discuss them.

❹ **Before You Move On** Work with your classmates. Write a "courtesy law" for your own classroom.

D WORD WORK

1. Word Detective Words that look alike, or almost alike, often belong to the same word family. Read this list of verbs. Write a noun that is a family member for each verb. Use your dictionary for help.

1. require   _requirement_
2. argue   _____
3. respect   _____
4. learn   _____
5. create   _____
6. decide   _____

2. Word Study Members of the same word family look almost alike, but they have different meanings and different jobs in a sentence. Make up another sentence for each of these words.

VERB	NOUN	ADJECTIVE
require	requirement	required
Ms. Chiu's class requires a lot of homework.	Homework is a requirement.	Science is a required class.

SPELLING AND PHONICS: To do this activity, go to page 196.

3. Word Play Work with a partner. Complete the following word family chart. Use your dictionary for help. Then choose two of the word families and write a sentence for each word (6 sentences).

Verb	Noun	Adjective
create	_creation_	creative
decision	decisive	
writing	written	
respect	respect	
paint		painted
harm		harmful

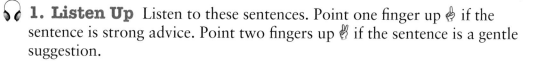

E GRAMMAR — Using Modals to Persuade Others

1. Listen Up Listen to these sentences. Point one finger up 👆 if the sentence is strong advice. Point two fingers up ✌️ if the sentence is a gentle suggestion.

👆 ✌️ 1. You should obey your teacher.

👆 ✌️ 2. You could try to study harder.

👆 ✌️ 3. You might try to study harder.

👆 ✌️ 4. If you study harder, you may get a better grade.

👆 ✌️ 5. If you want others to like you, you will be kind to them.

👆 ✌️ 6. You can get good grades if you study hard.

2. Learn the Rule Imagine you want to convince someone to do what you say. Certain modals can help you do this. Read the following rules, then do Activity 1 again.

USING MODALS TO PERSUADE OTHERS
1. When you want to give advice, use *should*. The advice can sometimes sound like a command:
*You **should** treat others with respect. You **shouldn't** be rude to others.*
2. When you want to give someone a good reason for doing something (or not doing something), use modals like **can, may, could,** or **might.** These modals all express possibility:
*Skateboarding **can** be dangerous. If you go too fast, you **may** fall. If you fall, you **might** break a leg. If you break your leg, you **could** end up with a cast.*
3. The modal **will** is stronger. It expresses strong probability or certainty:
*If your leg is in a cast, you **won't** be able to dance. You **will** catch cold if you don't put on a coat.*
4. Do not use these modals (except **will**) in an *if* clause. That's because *if* already expresses possibility—
Right: *If you break your leg, you will have to wear a cast.*   Wrong: *If you ~~might~~ break your leg, you will have to wear a cast.*

3. Practice the Rule Write one sentence for each modal: *can, may, could, might, will, should.*

F | BRIDGE TO WRITING

Feature Articles: Debates

1. Before You Read Make a list of five common foods that kids often eat for lunch. Circle the foods on your list that are good for you (healthy).

 2. Let's Read Skim the first paragraph for examples of foods that are bad for you, or junk food. Then skim for information about why these foods are unhealthy.

Ban Junk Food in School? (Debate)

1 Instead of eating a nutritious cafeteria lunch each day, Nicole Talbott grabs junk food. "Lunch for me is chips, soda, and maybe a chocolate ice-cream taco," the high-school student from Oakland, California, told The New York Times.

2 U.S. school officials say that students have too much sugar and fat in their diets. Many doctors agree. The number of overweight children and adolescents has more than doubled since the early 1970s.

3 As a result of such concerns, Nicole's school district and others across the U.S. have banned junk food. What do you think? Should junk food be banned in school?

YES

4 Junk food is especially harmful to growing kids. A recent study showed that half of the calories U.S. children consume come from fat and sugar. A can of soda, for example, contains 10 teaspoons of sugar!

5 "Schools should sell healthy food," says Jameela Syed, 10, a fifth-grader at Huth Road Elementary School in Grand Island, New York. "Healthy food can make you work better."

6 Banning junk food from schools—and teaching kids to eat right and exercise—will help students stay healthy.

NO

7 Making choices is an important part of learning. Deciding whether to eat junk food is one such decision.

8 "I think kids should be taught to be responsible, and they should learn about eating properly in health class," says Meghan Stubblebine, 14, a student at Canevin Catholic High School in Pittsburgh, Pennsylvania. "But kids should be able to choose what they eat."

9 Junk food may be bad for you, but deciding what to eat is a choice that students—not states or school districts—must make.

Source: *Junior Scholastic*

> Facts are used to back up the argument.

> Quotes help make the case, too.

> The word *but* tells you the writer is about to disagree!

official—someone who has an important job in an agency or business

school district—an agency that runs the schools

calories—the amount of energy in food. Too many calories make you gain weight.

consume—to eat

contain—to have something inside or to include something

responsible—making good choices

3. Making Content Connections You have read two articles about interesting issues. Work with a partner. Compare the articles. Complete the chart below.

	Courtesy Law	Ban Junk Food
1. What is the question?	*Should there be a law that requires students to be polite?*	
2. What are the arguments for answering *yes*?		
3. What are the arguments for answering *no*?		
4. What is your own answer to the question? Do you agree?		

4. Expanding your vocabulary. Work with a partner. Imagine that you are discussing or debating with classmates. Match the goals with the words you might say.

Goals	Words You Might Say
1. State your position	a. That's a good point, however …
2. Disagree with others	b. For example…
3. Try to understand better	c. I believe that…
4. Find out if others agree	d. Do you agree?
5. Try to convince others	e. Could you give me an example?
6. Support your position	f. It is important that…

G | WRITING CLINIC

1. Think about It In a newspaper, where would you most likely find articles like the ones in this unit?

☐ on the front page   ☐ on the editorial page   ☐ in the comics section

2. Focus on Organization

❶ Take another look at the debate about courtesy laws:

> *Making the title a question makes me want to read the article.*

Do Students Need a Courtesy Law? (Debate)

In Louisiana's public schools, being polite to teachers isn't just expected—it's required by state law. In 1999, Louisiana passed the first student respect law. It requires students to address their teachers as "sir" or "ma'am," or with appropriate titles, such as "Mrs." or "Mr."

"Just as we teach reading and writing, I think we can teach manners," says Donald Cravins, the state senator who sponsored the law.

The idea has spread quickly. Several other states are considering similar laws. But not everyone agrees that courtesy laws are a good idea. What do you think? Should students be required by law to be polite? Read both arguments, then decide.

Yes, Ma'am!

Teachers don't get enough respect from students today. Courtesy laws will help students and teachers work together to create an environment that fosters creativity and learning.

With courtesy laws in effect, teachers can spend less time disciplining their students and more time teaching them. "I've had teacher after teacher tell me that it's changed the whole experience in the classroom," says Louisiana Governor Mike Foster.

Many students agree that some kids need to learn better manners. "I think a courtesy law would help some kids show respect at home," says Kurt Phelan.

The beginning of the article gives us background information.

A quote helps focus on the debate.

*This paragraph states the **issue**.*

*Here is **one argument**.*

*Here is a **second argument**.*

*Here is a **third argument**.*

❷ Reread the other side of the debate. Outline the arguments. Add one more argument of your own.

No, Sir!

Good manners should be taught at home by parents, not in the schools. "Teachers deserve respect because they are adults," says 17-year old Peter Lainey. "But that decision should be left up the parents."

These kinds of laws only take attention away from the real problems that plague schools today. School districts need to build better schools, reduce drop-out rates, improve test scores, and raise teachers' salaries to really improve education.

"'Yes, ma'am' and 'no, ma'am' is fine, says Sue Hall, a teacher in New Orleans. "But it's pretty superficial. You're not getting to the root of the problem."

NO, there shouldn't be a law... _____.

Argument #1: _Good manners should be_

taught at home. _____.

Argument #2: _____

_____.

Argument #3: _____

_____.

Your own argument: _____

_____.

---

3. Focus on Style

❶ People's actual words, or quotes, often help support an argument.

"Kid's should have to earn their allowance," argues one father. "It teaches responsibility."

❷ Write sentences using these people's actual words. Use quotes.

EXAMPLE: 1. *Sara Chu-Smith says, "Everyone should read for an hour every day."*

1.

Sara Chu-Smith, publisher

2.

DeMonde Edwards, basketball player

3.

Ms. Flores, English teacher

4.

Zaida Ruiz, ninth-grader

5.

Brendon Tse, parent

6.

Mona Park, 17 years old

H WRITER'S WORKSHOP — Feature Articles: Debates

Work with a partner. You are going to write a feature article for the "Debate" section in *Junior Scholastic Magazine*. You will both write the introduction. Then, one of you will write the "yes" part of the article, and the other will write the "no" part.

1. Getting It Out

❶ Choose an interesting topic. Select something that both of you—

- know about.
- care about.

1.

Should schools have dress codes?

2.

Should we have a closed campus at lunch?

3.

Do students have too much homework?

4.

Your own question!

❷ Talk about the topic. What is the issue? Write a question. Your question should—

- be one that other students will be interested in.
- have a "yes" and "no" answer.
- begin with "Should …"

EXAMPLE: *Should kids have to work for an allowance?*

Your Question: _____

❸ Talk it out. Brainstorm reasons that people might answer your question "yes" and reasons people might answer "no." Make a like this one.

Our question: *Should kids have to work for their allowance?*

Yes	No
It would help kids learn good spending habits.	

❹ Decide who will write the arguments "for" and who will write the arguments "against."

❺ Find out more. Talk to others.

1. Take a survey of your classmates.

2. Interview other students. Think of two or three questions to ask. Write down the exact words that people say.

> 1. Do you think kids should get an allowance? How much?
>
> 2. Is it a good idea for kids to have to work for their allowance? Why or why not?

3. Talk to two or three adults. Get their ideas.

4. Search the Internet for information and ideas.

2. Getting It Down

❶ Make an outline like the one below.

Title: _Should kids have to work for their allowance?_
_____

Introduction (background information): _____

Position for: _Kids should have to work for their allowance_ _____.

    Argument 1: _____

    Argument 2: _____

    Argument 3: _____

Position against: _Kids shouldn't have to work for their allowance._ _____

    Argument 1: _____

    Argument 2: _____

    Argument 3: _____

The question is really interesting. I can't wait to read the article!

❷ Write a draft of your article. Here is part of what Suanna and Graciela wrote.

Should Kids Work for Their Allowance?

About half the kids in our class get an allowance, according to a recent survey. Some parents think that kids should earn their allowance. Others disagree. "My mom says that I have a right to a weekly sum—just like I have a right to a roof over my head," fellow student Juan Ortiz told us. What do you think?

Yes, kids should earn their allowance

Paying kids an allowance helps them understand the connection between working and spending. "I have to do special chores to get paid," says Annie Lau. "That means that I'm much more careful about how I spend my allowance."

If kids have to work for their money, they will want to work harder. They will figure out what needs to be done instead of waiting to be told.

Parents have to work for money. Why shouldn't kids have to do this too?

No, kids shouldn't have to earn their allowance

Most kids have a lot of homework. They don't have time.

The girls give us background information. They use facts and a quote to begin the debate.

They include position statements.

They give arguments for each side.

3. Getting It Right Look carefully at your review. Use this guide to revise your paragraph.

Ask yourself...	How to check...	How to revise...
1. Does the title of our article use a good question?	Find out if another pair of students in class wrote about the same topic. Compare your titles (questions).	Turn your title into a question. Make your question more specific.
2. Does your introduction give the reader background information?	Reread your introduction. Highlight the sentences that set the scene.	Add new information or a quote.
3. Do we give at least three arguments "for" and "against"?	Put a number in front of each argument.	Ask if your partner has any other ideas. Add arguments.
4. Do we provide both facts and opinions? Do we use quotes?	Underline each fact. Put a wavy line under each quote.	Add a fact or a quote.

4. Presenting It Share your article with your classmates.

❶ Choose one person to read aloud the question (your title) and the background information (introduction).

❷ If you wrote the "yes" section, read your arguments aloud. Speak slowly and clearly.

❸ Now have the person who wrote the "no" side read his or her arguments.

Encourage your classmates to add their own opinions.

1. On Assignment Stage a "role-play" debate.

❶ Choose an interesting issue:

☐ Should there be separate schools for boys and girls?
☐ Should schools ban chewing gum?
☐ Should you have to wear bicycle helmets?
☐ Should there be a limit on homework?
☐ Should schools allow students from other schools to attend school dances?

❷ Choose one of these four roles and write it on a 3" × 5" index card.

1.

Student

2.

Parent

3.
Teacher

4.

Principal

❸ Form a small group with other students who have the same role.

1. Discuss what the person on your card would probably say about the issue.
2. Write a position statement—for or against.
3. List one or more arguments the person might use.

❹ As a class, have your debate. State your argument.

❺ After the debate, decide which group presented the best arguments. Discuss why.

2. Link to Literature

SHARED READING All teens can agree on one issue: They want and need a larger allowance. This poem will teach you how to get it! As you read, underline the verbs you do not know.

LET'S TALK

1. Look first at the verbs you have underlined. Work with a classmate to find the definitions of ten of them.
2. Choose five verbs from number 1. Write a sentence for each one.
3. How do you persuade your parents? List five verbs that work for you.

ABOUT THE AUTHOR

Andrea Shavick is an award-winning English author and poet. She has written ten books for kids as well as a number of non-fiction books for adults.

How to Successfuly Persuade Your Parents to Give You More Pocket Money
by Andrea Shavick

Ask, request, demand, suggest, cajole or charm
Ingratiate, suck up to, flatter, complement or smarm
Negotiate, debate, discuss, persuade, convince, explain
Or reason, justify, protest, object, dispute, complain
Propose, entreat, beseech, beg, plead, appeal, implore
Harass, go on about it, pester, whinge, whine, nag and bore
Annoy, insult, reproach, denounce, squeal, scream and shout
Go quiet, subdued, look worried, fret, brood, tremble, shiver, pout
Act depressed, downhearted, upset, snivel, sigh
Go all glum and plaintive, wobble bottom lip and cry
Sniff, sulk, grumble, stare at ceiling, mope, pine, stay in bed
Get cross, get angry, fume, seethe, fester, agitate, see red
Provoke, enrage, push, bully, aggravate and goad
Screech, smoke, burn up, ignite, spark,detonate, EXPLODE

And if all that doesn't work

Here are two little tricks
That should do it with ease

No 1: smile
No 2: say please.

Source: *Unzip Your Lips Again*

pocket money—(*British*) spending money

Mini-Unit: Note-Taking and Summarizing

Sometimes it's hard to understand and remember everything you hear or read at school. **Note-taking** and **summarizing** can help you do both.

A LISTENING AND TAKING NOTES

Always take notes when you listen to your teacher describe or explain something (unless your teacher tells you to "just listen").

1. Talk It Over Talk with a partner. Add five examples to the list below of when you might take notes in class.

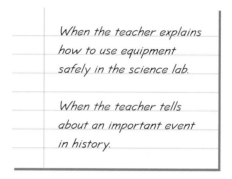

> When the teacher explains
> how to use equipment
> safely in the science lab.
>
> When the teacher tells
> about an important event
> in history.

2. Learn How to Do It Listening and note-taking is a six-step process. Read the steps below.

Step 1: Before class, make sure that you are *ready* to listen and learn. Do a quick check.
- I have done my homework and finished my assignments.
- I have reviewed yesterday's notes.
- I have my books and supplies.
- I intend, or *really mean*, to pay attention.

Step 2: Listen actively while others are talking. When you *listen*, you don't just hear words. You *think* about what the person is saying. You ask yourself questions.
- What am I learning?
- Why is this important or interesting to know?
- What do I need to remember?
- Do I understand what my teacher is explaining?

Step 3: Listen for "signal" words. They help you organize information.

First ... second ... third ... *in addition ...furthermore ... finally...*	*For instance ... for example ... picture this ... to illustrate...*	*Previously ... before ... at first ... as soon as ... following ... after...*
These signal that a **new idea** is coming.	These signal that an **example** is coming.	These let you know **when.**

Step 4: As you listen, write down ideas that are important. Jot down details, examples, definitions, and important facts that support each idea—

- Use your own words.
- Indent examples, details, and facts under each idea.
- Leave a wide margin on both sides of the paper.

2 inches		2 inches
	Grizzly bears are omnivores	
	-Love to eat small mammals, fish, and birds	
	-Also eat berries, roots, and other plants)	

Step 5: After class, review and edit your notes. <u>Underline</u> or highlight the most important ideas. Put a question mark ? next to points you don't understand. Add your own comments to your notes. Fill in missing points or define terms you need to remember.

Additional Notes		*Questions and Ideas*
	Grizzly bears are omnivores	
omnivore = eats both	*-Love to eat small mammals, fish, and birds*	*Do grizzly bears*
animals and plants	*-Also eat berries, roots, and other plants)*	*attack people?*

Step 6: Ask your teacher to explain the things you didn't understand.

🎧 **Practice It.** Listen to the passage. Take notes, then review them. Compare your own notes with a partner's notes.

When you read your textbook or are working on a report, take notes as you read to help you understand and remember what you read.

1. Talk It Over Talk with a partner. How can note-taking help you when you read? Add three ways to the list below.

Helps you really think about what you are reading.

---

2. Learn How to Do It *Graphic organizers* can help you take good notes. Remember to use your own words.

T-Charts

Use a **T-chart** when you are reading for **information**. Complete the T-chart below.

> Sharks are carnivores. They eat all kinds of flesh. Sharks prefer tuna, mackerel, and even smaller sharks for dinner, but they will eat swimmers if the conditions are right.
>
> Sharks have very sharp senses of vision, hearing, and smell to help them find food. They can see seven times better than humans and can hear sounds over two miles away. About two-thirds of a shark's brain is used for smell, so if there is even a tiny amount of blood in the water, a shark will smell it—even if it's almost a mile away!
>
> Instead of bones, sharks have something called cartilage. Bones are hard and don't bend. Cartilage is flexible, allowing sharks to bend so their heads can reach their tails. The cartilage also allows sharks to turn very quickly. All this makes them better hunters. Humans have cartilage too, but only in places like our ears and noses.

Ideas	Details, Examples
Sharks are carnivores (meat eaters)	They mostly eat smaller fish (tuna, mackerel, sharks)

Venn Diagrams

Use a **Venn diagram** when the reading is **comparing and contrasting** two things (describing how two things are the **same or different**). Make your own Venn diagram comparing alligators and crocodiles, based on this selection.

> In many ways, alligators and crocodiles are similar. They are both large reptiles that live in water and on land. They both lay eggs. They both have huge teeth and powerful jaws.
>
> But they are also different in many ways. The biggest difference between alligators and crocodiles is the shape of their heads. The crocodile's skull and jaws are long and narrow. The alligator's snout is flat and round. Alligators and crocodiles both have thick, bumpy skin but alligators tend to be darker in color.
>
> Another difference between crocodiles and alligators is their choice of homes. Alligators live in rivers, lakes, and swamps. On the other hand, crocodiles prefer coastal, salt water habitats.

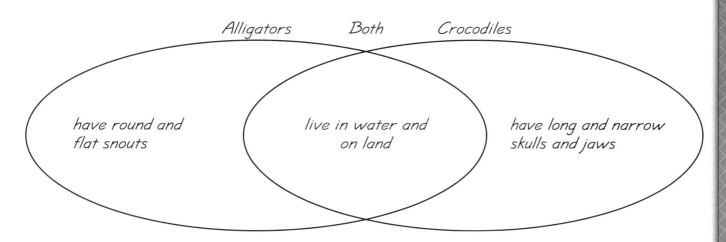

Alligators — Both — Crocodiles

have round and flat snouts

live in water and on land

have long and narrow skulls and jaws

Process Diagrams

When you are learning about a **step-by-step process**—like in science or health—use a **process diagram** that shows steps or stages.

> Have you ever wondered how you get cavities? The part of the tooth that you can see is called a crown. The crown of each tooth is covered with enamel, a very hard surface. Enamel protects the tooth. You have millions of bacteria, or very tiny germs, in your mouth. When you eat foods with sugar, like candy bars, the bacteria produce acids that eat through the enamel. The bacteria then get inside the tooth and cause it to decay. The decay can spread down into the tooth and cause it to die.

We have bacteria in our mouths. When we eat foods with sugar, the bacteria makes acids.

↓

Acids eat through the enamel (hard covering) of the tooth.

↓

Bacteria get inside the tooth and cause the tooth to decay.

Now practice making your own diagram. Read about why and how snow falls.

A cloud is a mixture of air and very tiny droplets of water. When the droplets of water get very cold, they turn to ice. Ice particles start very small. As they travel through the air, more water freezes on them, and they become larger, forming ice crystals. When the ice crystals are big enough, they join together and make snow flakes. If the snow flakes are heavy enough, they fall to the ground.

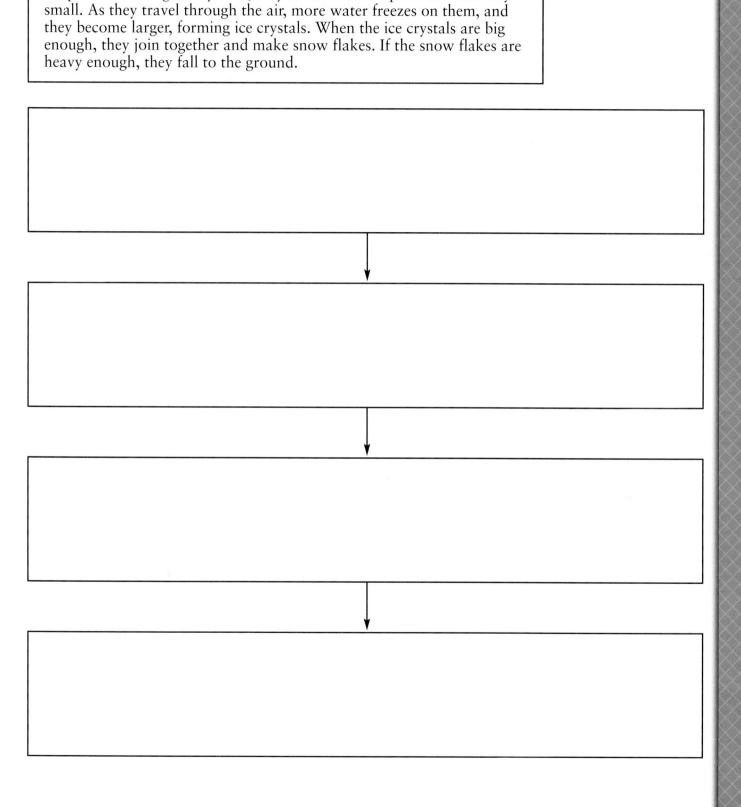

Timelines

When you are reading about an important **event in history**, make a **timeline**.
Read the passage and complete the timeline below.

> It is difficult to climb Mt. Everest. Many mountain climbers have died trying to reach the summit. In 1921, the first British team tried to reach the top. They couldn't make it, but they did discover a route to the summit. Many attempts followed. In 1924, British climbers George Mallory and Andrew Irvine attempted to climb Everest and were last seen just below the summit. No one knows if they reached the top before they disappeared. The first people we know reached the top were Edmund Hillary and his Sherpa guide, Tenzing Norgay, who succeeded in 1953. Both men became heroes. In 1980, the Austrian climber Rheinhold Messner climbed Mt. Everest alone—without bottled oxygen! He is considered by many to be the greatest mountain climber of all time.

1921	The first British team tried to climb Mt. Everest. They discovered a route, but didn't reach the top.
1924	George Mallory and Andrew Irvine tried to climb Mt. Everest. No one knows what happened to them.
1953	
1980	

3. Practice It Read these two passages. Decide which type of graphic organizer to use for each. Then take notes on a separate piece of paper. Compare your notes with a partner's.

Reading 1.

The Changing Look of America's Population

The United States is becoming more racially diverse than ever before. The most diverse group is people who are 18 years old and younger. Almost 40 percent of these people are members of a minority group, which in this case is a racial group smaller than the larger group that it belongs to.

Many Americans thought that America was becoming more diverse, but we weren't sure about it until the 2000 census was complete. A census is a count of the population of an area. Before 2000, people had to choose one race from a list of races to describe themselves in a census. But in Census 2000, people were allowed for the first time ever to choose more than one race. About 7 million people identified themselves as multiracial. Almost half of these people were 18 or younger than 18.

According to people who study population information and numbers, we are seeing increased racial diversity in the U.S. because of growing numbers of immigrants and interracial marriages here in the past several years.

Reading 2.

That volcano is about to erupt!

Do you know how and why a volcano erupts? To find out, we have to look inside the volcano. Under the ground, we find magma. Magma is hot, melted rock. Liquid magma moves around under the ground and can flow toward the surface inside a volcano. When this happens, the gas in the magma starts to bubble up, forcing the magma upward. If earthquakes happen near a volcano, you can be sure that the volcano is active because the upward movement of magma can cause earthquakes.

If you see the rocky top surface of a volcano bulging outward, run fast, because it means that gas and magma are collecting and the volcano might erupt. But before the eruption occurs, steam and gas will shoot out of cracks and holes in the volcano to release some of the pressure that's building up inside. When there is too much magma and gas to be released through these small cracks and holes, or if the top of the volcano breaks open because of an earthquake, the volcano will erupt, shooting out steam, ash, and sometimes lava, which is what magma is called when it reaches the surface.

READING AND SUMMARIZING

When you summarize, you find the most important ideas in something you've read, then *restate* them in your own words. Writing a summary shows how well you understand something.

1. Talk It Over Talk with a partner. Write down one reason that summarizing might help you in school. Be ready to share.

2. Learn How to Do It Read the passage. Then read the summary.

Reading Passage

The Changing Look of America's Population

The United States is becoming more racially diverse than ever before. The most diverse group is people who are 18 years old and younger. Almost 40 percent of these people are members of a minority group, which in this case is a racial group smaller than the larger group that it belongs to.

Many Americans thought that America was becoming more diverse, but we weren't sure about it until the 2000 census was complete. A census is a count of the population of an area. Before 2000, people had to choose one race from a list of races to describe themselves in a census. But in Census 2000, people were allowed for the first time ever to choose more than one race. About 7 million people identified themselves as multiracial. Almost half of these people were 18 or younger than 18.

According to people who study population information and numbers, we are seeing increased racial diversity in the U.S. because of growing numbers of immigrants and interracial marriages here in the past several years.

Summary

More and more kids in the U.S. belong to more than one race. For the first time, in the 2000 census, people were allowed to identify themselves as members of more than one racial group. About seven million people did this. This change is the result of an increase in immigration and interracial marriages.

How to summarize:

1. Read the passage, taking notes.
2. Review your notes, underlining the important ideas. Next, circle absolutely essential information.
3. Write a paragraph that includes the important ideas and details.

3. Practice It Summaries are short, and they are in your own words. You will need two pieces of paper for this activity. Number each one in the upper right hand corner. As you do the activity, be sure that your handwriting is the same size on each sheet.

1. Fold sheet #1 in half so you have a short, wide piece of paper. Read the passage below. Write down the most important ideas and details from the passage.
2. Fold sheet #2 in three parts so you have a very short, wide piece of paper. Study the notes on sheet #1, crossing off less important ideas or details. Then fill up sheet #2 with the notes that you think are the most important.
3. Use the notes from sheet #2 to write a short paragraph about the reading. Remember to write complete sentences and use your own words.

Why Egyptians Learned to Make Mummies

Ancient Egyptians believed that a person's soul lived on after a person died, but didn't stay near the body after death. Instead, it left its body after death and returned to find it later. The body needed its soul to go to the mythical Next World. But the *soul* couldn't return if it couldn't find or didn't recognize its body.

When Egyptians buried their dead in the sand, the hot, dry weather dried up the bodies and stopped them from rotting. But sand burials weren't good enough for wealthy Egyptians. They started to bury their family members in beautiful stone tombs. However, they soon realized that this was a horrible mistake because the bodies didn't dry up in the tombs like they did in the sand. They became skeletons. What would the Egyptians do? The souls wouldn't be able to recognize their bodies if the bodies turned into skeletons! These people would never be able to go to the Next World!

The wealthy Egyptians didn't want to go back to burying their loved ones in sand, but they had to solve this problem of bodies rotting away and becoming unrecognizable to their souls. They learned from the sand burials that bodies could be preserved if they were kept dry. They tried different things for many years until they finally discovered the perfect way to preserve bodies without burying them in the sand. They found a way to make mummies. Their techniques were so good that some of the mummified bodies still exist.

Spelling and Phonics Activities

🎧 UNIT 1

Spelling and Phonics The sound /ā/ can be spelled many ways, depending on the word it is in. Listen to the following words.

claim   fame   play   great   obey

Supply the missing letters for each incomplete word. Use your dictionary to check your work.

a. The team won the
   g_a_me.

b. Don't be l____te!

c. I got a letter in
   the m____l.

d. Please w____t for me.

e. Juan took the
   subw____.

f. My favorite food
   is st____k.

g. Let's t____ke
   a br____k.

h. This t____stes
   delicious.

i. I'm filling out a
   surv____.

🎧 UNIT 2

Spelling and Phonics The sound /ch/ can be spelled in many ways. Listen to the following words.

cockroach   kitchen   creature

Supply the missing letters for each incomplete word. Use your dictionary to check your work.

a. What time is it? I forgot my wa_tch_.

b. Here is a pic____re of my dog.

c. A ____impanzee is a kind of monkey.

d. I got a sunburn at the bea____.

e. You should stre____ before
   you exercise.

f. I want to see an adven____re movie.

UNIT 3

Spelling and Phonics The sound /ō/ can be spelled in many ways. Listen to the following words.

m**o**le   b**ow**l   s**oa**p   t**oe**   th**ough**

Supply the missing letters for each incomplete word. Use your dictionary to check your work.

a. Sh_ow_ me!

b. This car g____s fast.

c. Eeek! It's a gh____st!

d. I have a sore thr____t.

e. It's sn____ing.

f. Sl____ down!

g. It's a cockr____ch!

h. I wr____te the n____te.

i. Do you kn____ any j____kes?

j. I'm watching a talk sh____.

k. What's your zip c____de?

l. Roll the d____ into a ball.

UNIT 4

Spelling and Phonics In some words the letters -*gh*- are silent, and in some words they have a /f/ sound. Listen to the example sentence. Notice how the underlined words are pronounced.

Example: I thou**gh**t my old friends weren't cool enou**gh** for me.

Say the following words. Then put each one in the correct place in the chart.

cough	straight	neighbor	eight	light	tough
taught	laugh	high	thought	might	right
caught	height	night	through	bought	enough

-*gh*- is silent	-*gh*- sounds like /f/
eight	*cough*

UNIT 5

Spelling and Phonics The sound /o͞o/ can be spelled in many ways. Listen to the following words.

food   dude   chew   true   who   soup

Supply the missing letters for each incomplete word. Use your dictionary to check your work.

a. shamp__oo__   d. bl____   g. st____dent   j. z____

b. st____   e. r____de   h. gr____p   k. s____n

c. scr____   f. gl____   i. m____ve   l. y____

UNIT 6

Spelling and Phonics The letters -oo- can be pronounced in different ways. Listen to the following words.

took   blood   balloon   door

Say the following words. Then put each one in the correct place in the chart.

| flood | floor | moon | pool | look | poor |
| cookie | cool | good | school | cook | foot |

/o͝o/ as in *took*	/ŭ/ as in *blood*	/o͞o/ as in *balloon*	/ô/ as in *door*
cook			

Spelling and Phonics The letters -*ou*- can be pronounced in different ways. Listen to the following words.

found   thought   touch   group

Say the following words. Then put each one in the correct place in the chart.

cloud	country	youth	around	soup	out
through	pound	ground	enough	count	cough

/ou/ as in *found*	/ŏ/ as in *thought*	/ŭ/ as in *touch*	/o͞o/ as in *group*
cloud			

Spelling and Phonics The letters -*ea*- can be pronounced many ways. Listen to the following words.

health   great   tea

Say the following words. Then put each one in the correct place in the chart.

dead	ready	break	real	increase	headache
steak	beneath	creature	cheap	bread	deal

/ĕ/ as in *health*	/ā/ as in *great*	/ē/ as in *tea*
dead		

UNIT 9

Spelling and Phonics The sound /j/ can be spelled many ways, depending on the word it is in. Listen to the following words.

jelly   gigantic   fudge   age

Supply the missing letters for each incomplete word. Use your dictionary to check your work.

a. Tan____erines are sweet.

b. The police officer wears a ba____.

c. Would you like bacon or sausa____?

d. I put ____am on my toast.

e. My favorite drink is oran____ ____uice.

f. The tallest animal in the world is a ____iraffe.

UNIT 10

Spelling and Phonics The sound /or/ can be spelled many ways, depending on the word it is in. Listen to the following words.

for   more   four   board   floor

Supply the missing letters for each incomplete word. Use your dictionary to check your work.

a. Of c____se, I'll go with you.

b. Go to the blackb____d.

c. I didn't study, so I did a p____ job on my math test.

d. Please shut the d____.

e. She w____ a black dress.

f. I love to eat popc____n.

g. I live in New Y____k.

h. I heard a r____.

i. Let me p____ some milk for you.

ChecBrics*

ChecBric for Interview

Focus	Overall rating
Organization ____ My heading names the person and tells about their claim to fame. ____ I based my interview on questions and answers.	____ 4 = Wow! ____ 3 = Strong ____ 2 = Some strengths ____ 1 = Needs work
Content ____ My questions and answers are about the person's "claim to fame." ____ The interview tells facts the reader might not know about the person. ____ I used the person's exact words in each answer.	____ 4 = Wow! ____ 3 = Strong ____ 2 = Some strengths ____ 1 = Needs work
Style ____ I avoided asking questions with yes/no answers. ____ My questions were open-ended, so the person had to give details. ____ The answers sound like the person is talking to you.	____ 4 = Wow! ____ 3 = Strong ____ 2 = Some strengths ____ 1 = Needs work
Grammar and mechanics ____ I used complete sentences. ____ I used the correct word order for my questions. ____ I used helping verbs for my questions when needed. ____ I started each sentence with a capital letter and ended it with the correct punctuation.	____ 4 = Wow! ____ 3 = Strong ____ 2 = Some strengths ____ 1 = Needs work

ChecBric name and concept created by Larry Lewin.

ChecBric for Informational Report

Focus	Overall rating
Organization ____ My paragraph has a topic sentence. ____ I gave at least three details. ____ Each detail connects to the topic sentence.	____ 4 = Wow! ____ 3 = Strong ____ 2 = Some strengths ____ 1 = Needs work
Content ____ I used important information. ____ I used correct information. ____ The reader will learn new information.	____ 4 = Wow! ____ 3 = Strong ____ 2 = Some strengths ____ 1 = Needs work
Style ____ My paragraph will be easy for the reader to understand. ____ My paragraph "lives and breathes." ____ I used adjectives to paint a word picture.	____ 4 = Wow! ____ 3 = Strong ____ 2 = Some strengths ____ 1 = Needs work
Grammar and mechanics ____ I used complete sentences. ____ I made the verbs and subjects agree. ____ I indented my paragraph. ____ I used commas correctly. ____ I started each sentence with a capital letter and ended it with the correct punctuation.	____ 4 = Wow! ____ 3 = Strong ____ 2 = Some strengths ____ 1 = Needs work

ChecBric for How-to Instructions

Focus	Overall rating
Organization ____ I listed the necessary materials. ____ I used numbers to connect the steps. ____ I put the steps in time order.	____ 4 = Wow! ____ 3 = Strong ____ 2 = Some strengths ____ 1 = Needs work
Content ____ Each sentence is clear. ____ Each step is accurate. ____ Each sentence gives an important detail. ____ My instructions are easy to follow.	____ 4 = Wow! ____ 3 = Strong ____ 2 = Some strengths ____ 1 = Needs work
Style ____ My sentences are short and simple. ____ I used exact words. ____ I used the same words for things in every step.	____ 4 = Wow! ____ 3 = Strong ____ 2 = Some strengths ____ 1 = Needs work
Grammar and mechanics ____ I used complete sentences. ____ I used "do-it" sentences. ____ I started each sentence with a capital letter and ended it with the correct punctuation.	____ 4 = Wow! ____ 3 = Strong ____ 2 = Some strengths ____ 1 = Needs work

ChecBric for Personal Narrative

Focus	Overall rating
Organization ____ My story has a beginning that sets the scene. ____ I explained what happened. ____ I described the result.	____ 4 = Wow! ____ 3 = Strong ____ 2 = Some strengths ____ 1 = Needs work
Content ____ My story tells *who*, *what*, and *when*. ____ I explained why I did what I did. ____ I let the reader know how I felt.	____ 4 = Wow! ____ 3 = Strong ____ 2 = Some strengths ____ 1 = Needs work
Style ____ I told the story in an interesting way. ____ I talked to the reader like a friend. ____ I used casual, everyday words.	____ 4 = Wow! ____ 3 = Strong ____ 2 = Some strengths ____ 1 = Needs work
Grammar and mechanics ____ I used complete sentences. ____ I used the past tense correctly. ____ I indented my paragraphs. ____ I used commas after "when" clauses. ____ I started each sentence with a capital letter and ended it with the correct punctuation.	____ 4 = Wow! ____ 3 = Strong ____ 2 = Some strengths ____ 1 = Needs work

ChecBric for Explaining a Process

Focus	Overall rating
Organization _____ I gave the main idea in the first sentence. _____ I explained the steps in the food chain process.	_____ 4 = Wow! _____ 3 = Strong _____ 2 = Some strengths _____ 1 = Needs work
Content _____ My report accurately describes a food chain. _____ I named plants and animals in the food chain. _____ I used a flow diagram to help explain the information.	_____ 4 = Wow! _____ 3 = Strong _____ 2 = Some strengths _____ 1 = Needs work
Style _____ I used formal, serious language. _____ I used the correct names for plants and animals. _____ I used longer sentences when they made my writing smoother.	_____ 4 = Wow! _____ 3 = Strong _____ 2 = Some strengths _____ 1 = Needs work
Grammar and mechanics _____ I used complete sentences. _____ I used the present and past tenses correctly. _____ I indented my paragraphs. _____ I used commas to set off examples. _____ I started each sentence with a capital letter and ended it with the correct punctuation.	_____ 4 = Wow! _____ 3 = Strong _____ 2 = Some strengths _____ 1 = Needs work

ChecBric for True Story

Focus	Overall rating
Organization ____ I gave my story a creative title. ____ My story has a beginning that grabs the reader's attention. ____ I described the events in the order they happened. ____ My story has an ending.	____ 4 = Wow! ____ 3 = Strong ____ 2 = Some strengths ____ 1 = Needs work
Content ____ I named the people and gave details about the setting. ____ I explained why the situation was serious. ____ I gave important details about what the "hero" did.	____ 4 = Wow! ____ 3 = Strong ____ 2 = Some strengths ____ 1 = Needs work
Style ____ The beginning and ending of my story interest the reader. ____ I used action-packed verbs. ____ I used the hero's own words to make the story interesting.	____ 4 = Wow! ____ 3 = Strong ____ 2 = Some strengths ____ 1 = Needs work
Grammar and mechanics ____ I used complete sentences. ____ I used "when" clauses correctly. ____ I used the past tense correctly. ____ I used exclamation points at the end of some sentences, but I didn't overuse them. ____ I started each sentence with a capital letter and ended it with the correct punctuation.	____ 4 = Wow! ____ 3 = Strong ____ 2 = Some strengths ____ 1 = Needs work

ChecBric for Describing an Event: Eyewitness Account

Focus	Overall rating
Organization ____ My introduction sets the scene. ____ I described the event in the order things happened. ____ I described what it was like right after the event happened (the aftermath).	____ 4 = Wow! ____ 3 = Strong ____ 2 = Some strengths ____ 1 = Needs work
Content ____ My description tells *what*, *when*, *where*, *who*, and *how*. ____ I gave a minute-by-minute description. ____ My description makes the reader feel like he or she is there.	____ 4 = Wow! ____ 3 = Strong ____ 2 = Some strengths ____ 1 = Needs work
Style ____ I used sense words (taste, touch, smell, sight, sound). ____ I used action-packed verbs. ____ I used similes to make my writing interesting.	____ 4 = Wow! ____ 3 = Strong ____ 2 = Some strengths ____ 1 = Needs work
Grammar and mechanics ____ I used complete sentences. ____ I used the past tense correctly. ____ I used commas in connected sentences. ____ I started each sentence with a capital letter and ended it with the correct punctuation.	____ 4 = Wow! ____ 3 = Strong ____ 2 = Some strengths ____ 1 = Needs work

ChecBric for Persuasive Writing

Focus	Overall rating
Organization _____ My title explains what the topic is. _____ My first sentence gives my position or opinion on the topic _____ Each sentence gives information that makes my position stronger. _____ My last sentence sums up my position, telling the reader what to do.	_____ 4 = Wow! _____ 3 = Strong _____ 2 = Some strengths _____ 1 = Needs work
Content _____ I gave reasons for my position. _____ I gave facts and examples. _____ I gave the names of experts. _____ I corrected the incorrect thoughts many people have about the topic.	_____ 4 = Wow! _____ 3 = Strong _____ 2 = Some strengths _____ 1 = Needs work
Style _____ I used subheadings to help my reader. _____ I involved my reader by asking questions.	_____ 4 = Wow! _____ 3 = Strong _____ 2 = Some strengths _____ 1 = Needs work
Grammar and mechanics _____ I used complete sentences. _____ I used gerunds correctly. _____ I started each sentence with a capital letter and ended it with the correct punctuation.	_____ 4 = Wow! _____ 3 = Strong _____ 2 = Some strengths _____ 1 = Needs work

ChecBric for Evaluation

Focus	Overall rating
Organization _____ I explained which food I was reviewing in my introduction and gave my opinion about it. _____ I gave several reasons for my opinion. _____ I made a recommendation to the reader in my conclusion.	_____ 4 = Wow! _____ 3 = Strong _____ 2 = Some strengths _____ 1 = Needs work
Content _____ I described the food I was reviewing. _____ I gave evidence to support my opinion. _____ I explained why others might like the product.	_____ 4 = Wow! _____ 3 = Strong _____ 2 = Some strengths _____ 1 = Needs work
Style _____ My introduction makes others want to read my review. _____ My readers can "hear" me talking to them. _____ I used stand-out adjectives.	_____ 4 = Wow! _____ 3 = Strong _____ 2 = Some strengths _____ 1 = Needs work
Grammar and mechanics _____ I used complete sentences. _____ I used "if" clauses correctly. _____ I used commas after introductory adverbs. _____ I made sure that verbs agreed with their subjects. _____ I started each sentence with a capital letter and ended it with the correct punctuation.	_____ 4 = Wow! _____ 3 = Strong _____ 2 = Some strengths _____ 1 = Needs work

ChecBric for Feature Article: Debate

Focus	Overall rating
Organization ____ My title explains what the debate is about. ____ My introduction makes the reader interested in the issue and gives background. ____ I gave more than one argument for each position. ____ I gave my arguments and evidence in a logical and clear way.	____ 4 = Wow! ____ 3 = Strong ____ 2 = Some strengths ____ 1 = Needs work
Content ____ My arguments and reasons are good. ____ I gave facts and examples to support each reason. ____ I listed opinions, using quotes.	____ 4 = Wow! ____ 3 = Strong ____ 2 = Some strengths ____ 1 = Needs work
Style ____ I quoted other people to make my point stronger and to make my writing more interesting. ____ I used people's exact words.	____ 4 = Wow! ____ 3 = Strong ____ 2 = Some strengths ____ 1 = Needs work
Grammar and mechanics ____ I used complete sentences. ____ I used modals like *should*, *can*, *may*, *might*, *could*, and *will* correctly. ____ I used the right punctuation in sentences with quotes.	____ 4 = Wow! ____ 3 = Strong ____ 2 = Some strengths ____ 1 = Needs work

Glossary

UNIT 1

academic—connected to learning and studying

acting—playing someone in a movie or show

advice—an opinion about what to do or not do

be serious about—to care a lot about something

business—buying and selling things

career—a job you have trained for and will do a long time

CIA—Central Intelligence Agency

claim to fame—the main reason a person is famous

degree—proof you have finished a course of study at a school—usually a university

dreams—hopes for the future

eventually—one day

fan—a person who likes something or someone a lot

featured—having a part in (a movie or story)

handle—to deal with

in a different light—in a different way

old-timer—someone from the past

opportunity—a chance to do something that will be good for you

own[1]—to have something because you bought it

own[2]—belonging to a person

performing arts—music, dance, or drama

pursue—to do or try something

root for—to want someone (like a sports team) to win

shortstop—the position between second and third base

stallion—a male horse

stereotype—an idea about a person based only on their race, religion, ethnic group, etc.

UNIT 2

amazing—making someone feel very surprised

amazing—very surprising

appetite—hunger

attack—to try to hurt

creature—an animal

crevice—a narrow opening

dangerous—able to hurt or kill

daredevil—someone who isn't afraid to do dangerous things

dinosaur—a reptile that lived millions of years ago

disgusting—very unpleasant and sickening

equipped for—made for

exceptional—very special

feared—frightening to others

metal—a material like steel, tin, or iron

path—way

powerful—very strong

scatter—to run in different directions

scurry—to move fast

survive—to stay alive

warning—a sign of danger

withstand—to experience without damage

UNIT 3

assistant—a helper

bristle—a hair on a brush

corn syrup—a sweet syrup

cornmeal—ground, dried corn

cover—to put something on something else

dab—a tiny amount

dribble—to drip in tiny drops

gelatin—a jelly-like substance used in cooking

have (someone do something)—to ask (someone to do something for you)

lb.—pound

mix—to stir together

mole—a dark growth on the skin, like a wart

oz.—ounce

place—to put somewhere

remove—to take out of

repeat—to do again

roll—to make round

slather—to spread thickly

slump—to fall over

sob—a small cry

spread—to cover something all the way to the edges

sprinkle—to scatter tiny pieces

stretch—to make something longer or larger by pulling

tbs.—tablespoon

admit—to let someone into a group
all the rage—very popular
backfire—to have a surprising negative result
backfire—to have the opposite effect of what you want
bald—having no hair on the head
brand-name—made by a well-known company
carefree—easygoing
clique—a group that hangs out together
conceited—stuck-up
cuff— to turn up the bottom of pants legs
dig—to like or understand someone or something
ditch—to get rid of someone
go out for—to try to join a team
image—what other people think about you
immature—childish
impress—to make someone think you are important

in return—by other people
in—fashionable and cool
intelligent—smart
jive—jazz music or insincere talk
jock—someone who is good at sports
jump on the bandwagon—to do what is popular with most people at the moment.
mean—nasty
motto—what somebody believes
perm—to make hair curly using a chemical treatment
popular—having lots of friends; well-liked
Raggedy Ann—a type of doll with bright red-orange hair.
silly—dumb
tortured imitation—a bad copy
transform—to change completely
varsity team—the main school sports team

chain—a sequence of closely connected things
energy—a source of power or strength
cause—to make something happen
destroy—to put an end to
environment—the natural world around us
depend on—to need and rely on

caterpillar—an early stage of a butterfly; like a hairy worm
wren—a type of tiny bird
hawk—a type of meat-eating bird similar to an eagle
fuel—something that helps create energy
seaweed—a family of underwater ocean plants

ambush—a surprise attack
Appalachian Mountains—a chain of mountains running from Canada to Alabama
baby-sitter—someone who cares for a young child
blacksmith—someone who makes things with iron
bus stop—a place where a bus always stops
depths—areas deep under the ground
dishwasher—a machine for washing dishes
dismay—disappointment
distract—to call attention to something else
emergency—a serious situation that needs immediate action
first aid—emergency help for an injured person
hairbrush—a brush for the hair
hero—someone who is very brave; especially who risked his/her life
lawnmower—a machine for cutting grass
life-saving—saving someone's life
lumbering crew—workers who cut down trees

ogre—a monster that often eats people
paramedic—person trained to give medical help in an emergency
physical therapy—special treatment for injuries to the body
pressure—(1) urgent problems; (2) pressing hard on the body
ravine—a deep, narrow valley
reassure—to give comfort
Red Cross—an organization that helps injured people or disaster survivors
rescue—to save from danger
rumpus—a fight
save a life—stop someone from dying
settler—someone who move into a new region
stay calm—avoid getting overexcited
tragic—a situation that causes terrible destruction or death
tussle—a fight

UNIT 7

argue—to disagree with someone
bang—boom
beast—a wild animal
bunk beds—two beds that are attached, one on top of the other
cobblestone—a paving stone
dark—black
deathly—as quiet as death
demolished—completely destroyed
ear-splitting—very, very loud
every once in a while—sometimes
explode—to blow up into many pieces
fear—to be afraid
Great Spirit—God
hymn—a religious song
noisy—loud

piling—a heavy beam that supports a building at the water's edge
quiet—peaceful
restless—not able to keep still
rubble—crumbled rock, bricks, etc.
rumble—a deep, rolling sound
shock—a strong jolt
siren—a piece of equipment on police cars and fire engines that makes very loud warning sounds
slab—a thick piece of something hard, like cement
straw—dried wheat
subside—to die down or become less
swirl—to twist
throw—to toss
trolley—a streetcar

UNIT 8

abuse—to use something in a way that it should not be used
affect—to cause a change in something
bad breath—air from your mouth that smells bad
bloodshot eyes—red eyes
blurred vision—not seeing clearly
brain function—how the brain works
cancer—a serious disease in which cells in your body do not stop copying themselves
coma—a deep sleep that you can't come out of
confusion—when you are not thinking clearly
coughing—when you push air out of your throat with a rough sound
damage—to have a bad effect on something
discreet—careful not to tell information that you want to keep secret
dislike—to not like someone or something
drop-out—a kid who leaves school
fact—something that is completely true
fatal—causing death
feeling dizzy—when you feel like you might fall over
groovy—a word used in the 1960s meaning "cool"
health—the condition of your body

illegal—against the law
incomplete—not finished
inhalant—a drug you inhale, often fumes from products like glue or paint thinner
intoxication—when you are drunk
lack of coordination—when your body doesn't move right
look to—to be attracted to
nausea—a feeling like you want to vomit
nonsmoker—someone who doesn't smoke cigarettes
oxygen—the air you breathe to stay alive
performance—the act of doing something
permanent—lasting forever
persuade—to give someone good reasons for doing something or not doing it
phlegm production—coughing up slimy mucus from the lungs
risk—the chance something bad could happen
self-control—the ability to control what you say and do
self-image—how you see yourself
trip—an experience someone has when taking an illegal drug
unpopular—not having many friends

Ben and Jerry's—a popular brand of ice cream
benefit—a positive result
calcium—a type of mineral
carbonated—having many tiny bubbles
cholesterol—a substance in your blood that can cause heart disease
clever—original
Concord—a type of sweet, purple grape
crack a smile—to begin to smile
delicious—tasting good
explosion—a sudden increase in the number of something
favorite—something someone likes best
fiber—a substance in vegetables, fruits, and grains that help move food through your body
flavor—the taste of food or drink
goo—a thick and sticky substance
guarantee—to promise
hilarious—very, very funny
hooked—liking something a lot
humorous—funny

iron—a type of mineral
make a mad dash—to hurry
mineral—a substance that humans, animals, and plants need to grow
normally—usually
nutritious—having things that keep you healthy
reduce—to make less
refreshing—making someone feel less tired or hot
source—where something comes from
special—like no other
strep throat—an illness that causes a very sore throat
substance—matter or material
tingly—a slight stinging feeling
varieties—different types
vitamin—a substance in foods that helps you grow and stay healthy
wacky—very silly
yum—you say this when something tastes good.
zany—funny in an unusual way

argument—an explanation you give for what you believe
ban—to order that an activity must not happen
calories—the amount of energy in food. Too many calories make you gain weight.
choice—the right to choose something
consider—to think about voting for
consume—to eat
contain—to have in it
courtesy—polite behavior to other people
creativity—using your imagination to do things
discipline—punish
drop-out rates—the numbers of kids quitting school
environment—the situation or people that affect how you live, learn, or work
expected—considered to be the thing that people should do
foster—to help something happen
improve—to make better or more
law—rules in a country, state, or city that we must follow

manners—polite ways of behaving
official—someone who has an important job in an agency or business
plague—to cause trouble again and again
pocket money—(British) spending money
position—an opinion about something
reduce—to make smaller or less
required—having to do something because it is a law or rule
respect—being polite to someone because they are important
responsible—making good choices
root—the main or basic part
school district—an agency that runs the schools
senator—a member of the Senate, one of two groups that makes laws
sponsor—to push for (a new law)
superficial—not very important

Common Irregular Verbs

Simple Form	Past Form	Past Participle	Simple Form	Past Form	Past Participle
be	was/were	been	lay (= put)	laid	laid
beat	beat	beaten	lead	led	led
become	became	become	leave	left	left
begin	began	begun	let	let	let
bend	bent	bent	lie (= lie down)	lay	lain
bite	bit	bitten	lose	lost	lost
break	broke	broken	make	made	made
bring	brought	brought	mean	meant	meant
build	built	built	meet	met	met
buy	bought	bought	pay	paid	paid
catch	caught	caught	put	put	put
choose	chose	chosen	quit	quit	quit
come	came	come	read	read	read
cost	cost	cost	ride	rode	ridden
cut	cut	cut	ring	rang	rung
do	did	done	rise	rose	risen
draw	drew	drawn	run	ran	run
drink	drank	drunk	say	said	said
eat	ate	eaten	see	saw	seen
fall	fell	fallen	sell	sold	sold
feed	fed	fed	send	sent	sent
feel	felt	felt	set	set	set
fight	fought	fought	show	showed	shown
find	found	found	shut	shut	shut
fly	flew	flown	sing	sang	sung
forget	forgot	forgotten	sit	sat	sat
forgive	forgave	forgiven	sleep	slept	slept
get	got	gotten	speak	spoke	spoken
give	gave	given	spend	spent	spent
go	went	gone	stand	stood	stood
grow	grew	grown	swim	swam	swum
have	had	had	take	took	taken
hear	heard	heard	teach	taught	taught
hide	hid	hidden	tear	tore	torn
hit	hit	hit	tell	told	told
hold	held	held	think	thought	thought
hurt	hurt	hurt	throw	threw	thrown
keep	kept	kept	understand	understood	understood
know	knew	known	wake	woke	woken

Listening Script

A. 1. Tuning In. (page 4)

Reporter: We're talking today to Frankie Morales, the star of the TV show, *The Adventures of Max Jones*. How does it feel to be the star of a popular TV show?

Frankie: It's always been my dream to be on a TV show.

Reporter: Do you have a favorite hobby?

Frankie: Golf is my favorite thing.

Reporter: Your TV character, Max, is a genius. What about you? Do you get good grades?

Frankie: I get straight A's, but Max gets straight A-pluses.

Reporter: Is your family anything like the wacky family on the show?

Frankie: The family on *The Adventures of Max Jones* is real. A lot of families do weird things. My family's not perfect, either.

UNIT 2

A. 1. Tuning In. (page 22)

Narrator: Listen to the description. Name the animal that we are describing. This animal is a snake—a very poisonous snake! It has a rattle at the end of its tail. When it is scared or angry, it coils its body and lifts its head and tail off the ground. The tail moves back and forth, making a rattling sound. This snake uses its rattle to scare away people or other animals. If you don't move away, it may bite you with its two sharp teeth, called *fangs*! The fangs pump poison into the victim. The poison is deadly! That means it can kill a person!

UNIT 3

A. 1. Tuning In. (page 40)

Teacher: Tomorrow is our party. Let's check to see if we're ready. Who's on the refreshments committee? Raise your hand. Juan...Lourdes...Parveen. Let's see, what are we having?

Parveen: Vampire Punch!

Juan: And Eyeball Cookies!

Teacher: I'll make the cookies tonight at home. And I'll buy the ingredients for the punch. You three will need to do the rest...Don't forget to bring in the punch bowl. And, don't forget to bring in a large plate for the cookies. We'll also need napkins and paper plates. We can make the ice for the punch in the morning. We can use the freezer in the cafeteria.

Parveen: What about decorations?

Teacher: I have a surprise! Look!

Juan: A pumpkin?

Teacher: Yes. We're going to make a Jack-o'-lantern.

Juan and Parveen: Cool!

Teacher: OK, Get ready to write down these steps. Take notes as you listen. Here's how to make a Jack-o'-lantern.

First, I'll put the pumpkin on a sheet of newspaper. This is a messy job.

Then, I'll cut out the top of the pumpkin around the stem...

Next, I'll lift off the top...

And then, I'll scoop out the seeds. I'm just going to use my hands.

Next, let's see which side of the pumpkin is the best side for the face... Maybe this side... Now, I'm cutting out the eyes...carefully. And, then the nose... And now the mouth...There!

We'll put the Jack-o'-lantern on the refreshments table, in the center. Finally, we'll put a short candle in the bottom of the pumpkin, and light it. Then we'll turn out the lights.

Juan: That will be fun.

Teacher: It sure will. Remember to wear your costumes, everybody.

I. 1. On Assignment. (page 54)

See script for A.1.Tuning In. (page 40)

UNIT 4

A. 1. Tuning In. (page 58)

Lori: Michelle! You look so...*different*!

Michelle: Do you like it?

Lori: Uh...it's really...uh...*different*!

Michelle: Isn't it *cool*?

Lori: Uh...What do your parents think?

Michelle: They don't like it. But they say it's *my* hair and I can do what I want with it.

Lori: But, Michelle...the color...it's so...*blue*!

Michelle: Deep sky blue. It's called deep sky blue.

Lori: So...what made you dye your hair?

Michelle: All the girls are doing it...that is, all the girls who are really *cool*.

Lori: *Really*?

Michelle: Yeah! You should try it, Lori. You would look so cool with maybe...*green* hair...

Lori: But I *like* my hair ...

Michelle: Trust me. Black hair is *not* cool. You would look very cool with green hair! You'd have a lot more friends.

UNIT 5

A. 1. Tuning in. (Page 76)

There once was a flower that grew on the plain,
Where the sun helped it grow, so did the rain ...

There once was a bug who nibbled on flowers,
Nibbled on flowers for hours and hours!

The bug ate the flower that grew on the plain,
Where the sun helped it grow, so did the rain ...

There once was a bird who gobbled up bugs,
And creepies and crawlies, and slimies and slugs.

The bird ate the bug, who nibbled on flowers,
Nibbled on flowers for hours and hours!

The bug ate the flower that grew on the plain,
Where the sun helped it grow, so did the rain ...

There once was a snake who often grabbed birds,
And swallowed them whole, or so I have heard.

The snake ate the bird, who gobbled up bugs,
And creepies and crawlies, and slimies and slugs.

The bird ate the bug, who nibbled on flowers,
Nibbled on flowers for hours and hours!

The bug ate the flower that grew on the plain,
Where the sun helped it grow, so did the rain ...

There once was a fox, and I'll make a bet:
He'd eat anything he could possibly get.

The fox ate the snake, who often grabbed birds,
And swallowed them whole, or so I have heard.

The snake ate the bird, who gobbled up bugs,
And creepies and crawlies, and slimies and slugs.

The bird ate the bug, who nibbled on flowers,
Nibbled on flowers for hours and hours!

The bug ate the flower that grew on the plain,
Where the sun helped it grow, and so did the rain...

A. 1. Tuning In. (page 94)

Amanda: My best friend Carmen and I were playing in the middle of a lake with some other friends when we heard a huge splash. Suddenly, Carmen disappeared. She just went under. I was really scared, but I couldn't just leave her!

Underwater, a huge alligator—it was at least ten or eleven feet long—was spinning Carmen around and around and it had her arm clenched in its jaws. It felt like a tornado! Suddenly the 'gator let her go, and I knew it was now or never!

The alligator started swimming toward us again. The other kids raced to the shore, screaming. I pulled Carmen onto a boogie board. We were terrified! We kicked about 150 feet back to shore.

The 'gator had broken Carmen's arm and ripped a seven-inch gash in her skin, but it could have been worse!

Carmen: If Amanda hadn't saved me, the alligator probably would have won! She's my hero!

H. 1. Getting It Out, Part 3. (page 104)

Interviewer: What's your name?
Karla: Karla Pierce.
Interviewer: What did you do, Karla?
Karla: I saved my dog's life. I saved him from drowning.
Interviewer: Where did it happen?
Karla: In my backyard. We have a stream that runs behind our house.
Interviewer: So, tell me what happened.
Karla: Well, my family had friends over. We were having a barbecue in the backyard. Suddenly, someone shouted that our dog Tucker was in the stream.
Interviewer: Does he know how to swim?
Karla: He *does*, but the stream was moving really, really fast.
Interviewer: I see. So what did you do?

Karla: I rushed to the edge of the stream and saw that Tucker was in trouble. As I said, the stream was moving really fast. He was fighting the water and kept hitting the rocks. So I stretched out on the side of the stream—it was really slippery—and hooked my foot around a tree. I reached out over the water and grabbed Tucker by the paw. I pulled him out of the water. He weighs at least 100 pounds!
Interviewer: Did everything turn out OK?
Karla: We were both cold, muddy, and wet, but we were OK.
Interviewer: You must have been scared!
Karla: I was really scared. I knew that if I didn't do something, Tucker might drown. Sometimes you have to try your hardest and not give up, you know.

H. 1. Getting It Out, Part 5. (page 105)

Interviewer: What's your name?
Aaron: Aaron Wallace.
Interviewer: And how old are you, Aaron?
Aaron: I'm 16.
Interviewer: Where do you live?
Aaron: In Virginia.
Interviewer: Tell me what happened.
Aaron: Well, I was walking home from school, and I saw Amber and her cousin playing on the train tracks.
Interviewer: How old are they?
Aaron: Amber's about two and her cousin is four.
Interviewer: Please, go on.
Aaron: I've been around trains my whole life, so I know that train tracks are a

dangerous place to play. I sensed a train was coming. I told the kids to leave the track, but only Amber's cousin did.

Suddenly, I saw a train coming around the curve. I grabbed Amber in my arms. Then I heard her mom. She was yelling, "Jump! Jump!" I held Amber really tight and jumped off the tracks. The train roared by right at that second!
Interviewer: So, then what happened?
Aaron: The train company gave me an award. They said I was courageous. I don't really feel like that, though. I think anyone would have done the same thing.

A. 1. Tuning In. (page 112)

Teenage Boy: It happened last summer. We were on a Boy Scout camping trip. All of a sudden, we heard the news. It was headed toward us! Soon it would hit!

The wind started to blow. Things started flying around. The sky turned nasty gray. Everybody was running around with their ponchos flying in the wind.

The wind got stronger. Lawn chairs started flying by. The flagpole at our camp site came down. By now, it was really raining hard. Our tents started blowing away.

Then it was over. The sky got brighter. The wind died down, and the rain stopped.

It was incredible!

Woman: I was making dinner when the first shock came. The house started to shake. Then it got stronger. Pictures fell off the wall. Our TV crashed to the floor. Dishes started to break.

I grabbed the kids, and we ran outside. We all crawled under a picnic table. Another shock came, and we saw the chimney fall off the roof. Horrible sounds came from the house—crashing sounds, creaking, groaning. Then it was quiet. Nobody said a word. We just hoped it was over!

Girl: When I got up that morning, I saw black clouds in the sky. By noon, it was starting to rain and by late afternoon it was raining really hard. My friend Ann and I decided to walk into town. Big mistake! In the five minutes that it took us to get into town, the rain became sheets of water.

The streets turned to rivers. Cars couldn't move, and drivers were trapped in their cars. We were standing in water up to our waists. We were trapped!

A. 1. Tuning In. (page 130)

Amy: Hey, Maria, let's have a beer. It's Saturday night. My mom and dad are gone. We can do anything we want here.

Maria: Amy, I don't think we should. What if they come home? What if they find out?

Amy: Look, it's not like drugs. Our parents drink. Why shouldn't we?

Maria: Our parents are adults. We're only 16. Besides, alcohol is bad for you. It can make you sick. It can make you lose control.

Amy: Look, one beer isn't going to kill you, Maria.

Maria: Stop trying to pressure me, Amy. If you want to drink so badly, go find another friend. I'm going home.

Amy: Wait, Maria, don't go. I'm sorry. I didn't mean to pressure you.

UNIT 9

A. 1. Tuning In. (page 148)

Speaker Number 1

This is my favorite food! I love it with a soft and chewy crust and when it's covered with lots of stringy cheese. When it comes out of the oven, you can smell the tomato sauce and the spices.

Speaker Number 2

Instead of a candy bar or potato chips, I have one of these when I get home from school. It's sweet and tasty and crunchy to eat. And, it's healthy, too.

Speaker Number 3

I love this in desserts like pie and cake, but I wouldn't want to eat it all by itself. It can be so sour! It can make your mouth pucker!

Speaker Number 4

I love to have this on a hot, summer day. It's cold and kind of creamy. I love to make it with raspberries or bananas.

Speaker Number 5

Sometimes I put this on toast or crackers. It can be smooth or crunchy. It's fun to eat because it sticks to the roof of your mouth.

Speaker Number 6

This comes from a chicken. It's sort of round and it's runny if you break it. You can fry it, scramble it, or boil it. I have one of these nearly every morning for breakfast.

UNIT 10

A. 1. Tuning In. (page 166)

Erik: Mom, can I have an allowance?

Erik's mother: An allowance? How much do you want?

Erik: Twenty dollars a week.

Erik's mother: Twenty dollars! That's a lot!

Erik: It isn't! I need to buy things for school. All of my friends get an allowance...!

Erik's mother: Well...maybe you can have an allowance, but you'll have to earn it. You'll have to work for it.

Erik: Earn it? You mean do things around the house, like making my bed...and taking out the garbage...and clearing the table after dinner?

Erik's mother: I *expect* you to do *those* things! No, I mean special jobs. If you get an allowance, you will need to do things like wash the windows and paint the garage.

Erik: That's not fair!

Erik's mother: It *is* fair. Kids should work for their allowance. Work teaches you the value of money.

Erik: But I have so much homework! And I have sports after school. I don't have time to wash the windows or paint the garage!

Erik's mother: Too bad. Your father and I both have to work for our money. You should have to work, too.

MINI-UNIT

Let's talk about the grizzly bear.

A large grizzly bear is one of the strongest animals in the world. A full-grown male is over eight feet long from nose to tail and can weigh over 700 pounds. Grizzlies are omnivores. They eat everything from squirrels to deer, and from berries to birds. Almost any animal in grizzly country may wind up as a meal for this mighty hunter.

There is no doubt that a grizzly bear is a dangerous animal and should be left alone. If you see a bear that is far away or doesn't see you, turn around and go back. If the bear is close or does see you, remain calm. Do not run. Instead, stand tall or back away slowly and wave your hands and speak loudly. The chances are that the bear will not bother you and will disappear.

Index

Text and Audio Credits

p. 24 From "Cockroaches," *The Unhuggables* by Victor Waldrup, Debbie Anker, and Elizabeth Blizzard. Copyright © 1988 National Wildlife Federation. Used by permission; *p. 28* "Sharks" from *Animals Nobody Loves* by Seymour Simon. Copyright © 2001 by Seymour Simon. Used with permission of Chronicle Books LLC, San Francisco. Visit Chronicle Books.com. Audio reproduced by permission of the Wendy Schmalz Agency; *p. 37* "Acro-Bat" copyright © 1997 by Kenn Nesbitt. Reprinted and reproduced by permission of the author. www.poetry4kids.com. All rights reserved. *pp. 42, 48* "Create Your Own Halloween Makeup," *National Geographic World*, October 2000. Used by permission of National Geographic Society; *p. 46* "Lose Your Head," *National Geographic Kids*, October 2002. Used by permission of National Geographic Society; *p. 54* Recipe for "Eyeballs" courtesy of BlackDog - The Site for Kids! Visit BlackDog on the World Wide Web: www.blackdog.net; *p. 55* "Best Mask?" from *Falling Up* by Shel Silverstein. Copyright © 1996 by Shel Silverstein. Used by permission of HarperCollins Publishers; *pp. 60, 64* © 2001 by Consumers Union of U.S., Inc., Yonkers, NY 10703-1057, a nonprofit organization. Reprinted and reproduced with permission from *Zillions: CONSUMER REPORTS® for Kids* Online for educational purposes only. No commercial use or reproduction permitted. www.zillions.org, http://www.zillions.org and www.ConsumerReports.org, http://www.ConsumerReports.org; *p. 73* "Motto" from *The Collected Poems of Langston Hughes* by Langston Hughes, copyright © 1994 by The Estate of Langston Hughes. Used by permission of Alfred A. Knopf, a division of Random House, Inc. and Harold Ober Associates Incorporated; *p. 78* Adapted from *Who Eats What?* by Patricia Lauber, HarperCollins, 1995; *p. 94* "Kids Did It! Real-Life Heroes" by Robin Terry from *National Geographic Kids*, October 2002. Used by permission of National Geographic Society; *p. 96*, "Calm Under Pressure" by Laura Daily from *National Geographic World*, July 2000. Used by permission of National Geographic Society; *p. 100* "'Bear-ly in Time" by Laura Daily from *National Geographic World*, July 2000. Used by permission of National Geographic Society; *pp. 105-107* "Dog Catcher" by Laura Daily from *National Geographic World*, July 2000. Used by permission of National Geographic Society; *p. 105* "Leap of Faith" by Laura Daily from *National Geographic World*, July 2000. Used by permission of National Geographic Society; *p. 109* "Paul Bunyan and the Gumberoos" from *Paul Bunyan* by Steven Kellogg. Text copyright © 1984 by Steven Kellogg. Used by permission of Harper Collins Publishers; *p. 114* "I Survived a Tornado!" from "Twister: winds of fury" by Jerry Dunn, *National Geographic World*, May 1997. Used by permission of National Geographic Society; *p. 118* Adaptation of "Thomas Jefferson Chase's account of the 1906 San Francisco earthquake," www.sfmuseum.org. Used by permission of The Virtual Museum of San Francisco; *p. 127* Adapted from "The Turtle Tale." Reprinted and reproduced with permission from *Earthquakes*, copyright © 1989, National Science Teachers Association and the Federal Emergency Management Agency; *p. 132* From the Coalition for Drug-Free City. *p. 145* Reprinted and reproduced with the permission of Simon & Schuster Books for Young Readers, an imprint of Simon & Schuster Children's Publishing Division from *Go Ask Alice* by Anonymous. Copyright © 1971 Simon & Schuster, Inc.; *p. 150* "Jello-O" by Casey D., *Teen Ink Reviews*. Reprinted and reproduced by permission from *Teen Ink* Magazine and teenink.com; *p. 154* From of "Oatmeal" by Keith R., *Teen Ink Reviews*. Reprinted and reproduced by permission from *Teen Ink* Magazine and teenink.com; *p. 163* Review of *Falling Up* by Shel Silverstein written by Amy P., *Teen Ink Book Reviews*. Reprinted and reproduced by permission from *Teen Ink* Magazine and teenink.com. Used by permission; *p. 163* "Tattooin' Ruth" from *Falling Up* by Shel Silverstein, HarperCollins, 1996; *p. 168* "Do Students Need a Courtesy Law?" from *Junior Scholastic*, March 12, 2001. © 2001 by Scholastic Inc. Reprinted and reproduced by permission of Scholastic Inc.; *p. 172* "Ban Junk Food in School?" from *Junior Scholastic*, September 6, 2002. © 2002 by Scholastic Inc. Reprinted and reproduced by permission of Scholastic Inc.; *p. 181* "How to Successfully Persuade Your Parents to Give You More Pocket Money" by Andrea Shavick . © Andrea Shavick. First published in *Unzip Your Lips Again*, Macmillan Children's Books UK , 2000. Used by permission of the author.

Photo Credits

Cover Images: All cover images courtesy of the Getty Images Royalty-Free Collection except the following: cockroaches eating crackers: David Maitland/Getty Images; tropical storm: Images produced by Hal Pierce, Laboratory for Atmospheres, NASA Goddard Space Flight Center/NOAA; interview in classroom: Barbara Stitzer/Photo Edit; Frog: Royalty-Free/CORBIS; Giraffes: Royalty-Free/CORBIS; man caught in hurricane: Royalty-Free/CORBIS; California State Capitol: Focus Group/Andre Jenny/PictureQuest.

Interior Images: **From the Getty Images Royalty-Free Collection:** *p.* 20, bottom; *p.* 22, top left; *p.* 22, top middle; *p.* 29, row 1, photo 1; *p.* 29, row 1, photo 2; *p.* 29, row 1, photo 3; *p.* 29, row 2, photo 3; *p.* 29, row 3, photo 1; *p.* 29, row 3, photo 2; *p.* 29, row 3, photo 3; *p.* 32, photo 1; *p.* 32, photo 4; *p.* 57; *p.* 77, photo 2; *p.* 77, photo 3; *p.* 80, photo c; *p.* 80, photo e; *p.* 80, photo f; *p.* 86, photo a; *p.* 86, photo b; *p.* 86, photo c; *p.* 86, photo d; *p.* 90, photo 1; *p.* 90, photo 2; *p.* 90, photo 5; *p.* 90, photo 6; *p.* 90, photo 7; *p.* 90, photo 8; *p.* 90, photo 9; *p.* 91; *p.* 127; *p.* 154; *p.* 158, photo 1; *p.* 158, photo 3; *p.* 158, photo 4; **From the Corbis Royalty-Free Collection:** *p.* 4, bottom right; *p.* 29, row 1, photo 4; *p.* 77, photo 1; *p.* 77, photo 4; *p.* 80, photo b; *p.* 90, photo 4; *p.* 90, photo 10; *p.* 110, top; *p.* 112, photo 2; *p.* 112, photo 3; *p.* 112, photo 4; *p.* 112, photo 5; *p.* 122, top left; *p.* 122, top right; *p.* 122, bottom left; *p.* 122, bottom right; **Other Images:** *p.* 2, top: Peter Muhly/Reuters/CORBIS; *p.* 2, bottom: Paul Fenton/ZUMA Press; *p.* 4, top left: Frank Trapper/CORBIS; *p.* 4, top right: Darren Hauck/CORBIS; *p.* 4, bottom left: Reuters/CORBIS; *p.* 6: Peter Muhly/Reuters/CORBIS; *p.* 10: Paul Fenton/ZUMA Press; *p.* 19: Photodisc/PictureQuest; *p.* 20, top: David Maitland/Getty Images; *p.* 21: Romilly Lockyer/Getty Images; *p.* 22, top right: Jeremy Woodhouse/Getty Images; *p.* 22, bottom left: Davies & Starr/Getty Images; *p.* 22, bottom middle: S. J. Vincent/Getty Images; *p.* 22, bottom right: Mike Buxton; Papilio/CORBIS ; *p.* 23: Eldad Rafaeli/CORBIS; *p.* 24: David Maitland/Getty Images; *p.* 28: Romilly Lockyer/Getty Images; *p.* 29, row 1, photo 5: Arthur Morris/CORBIS; *p.* 29, row 2, photo 1: Geoff Du Feu/Getty Images; *p.* 29, row 2, photo 2: Staffan Widstrand/CORBIS; *p.* 32, photo 2: Mike Buxton; Papilio/CORBIS ; *p.* 32, photo 3: Paul A. Zahl/Getty Images; *p.* 55: Jeff Albertson/CORBIS; *p.* 60: Digital Vision/PictureQuest; *p.* 73, left: CORBIS; *p.* 73, right: Bettmann/CORBIS; *p.* 77, top: Zigy Kaluzny/Getty Images; *p.* 78: Photodisc/PictureQuest; *p.* 78: Ingram/PictureQuest; *p.* 80, photo a: Vera Storman/Getty Images; *p.* 80, photo d: Michael & Patricia Fogden/CORBIS; *p.* 80, photo g: iStockphoto / Patti Meador; *p.* 80, photo h: Johnathan Smith; Cordaiy Photo Library Ltd./CORBIS; *p.* 82: liquidlibrary/PictureQuest; *p.* 82: Stockbyte/PictureQuest; *p.* 90, photo 3: Cameron Read/Getty Images; *p.* 96: Swim Ink/CORBIS; *p.* 98: Susan Werner/Getty Images; *p.* 100: Digital Vision/PictureQuest; *p.* 100: Creatas/PictureQuest; *p.* 109: Michael Leslie; *p.* 110, bottom: CORBIS; *p.* 111: Michael Maslan Historic Photographs/CORBIS; *p.* 112, photo 1: CORBIS; *p.* 112, photo 6: Chris Butler/Photo Researchers, Inc. ; *p.* 146, top: Paul Poplis /Getty Images; *p.* 146, bottom: Leigh Beisch/Getty Images; *p.* 147: Paul Poplis /Getty Images; *p.* 158, photo 2: Richard Jung/Getty Images; *p.* 163: Jeff Albertson/CORBIS; *p.* 172: Brand X Pictures/PictureQuest; *p.* 181: Photo courtesy of Andrea Shavick.

Map of Central and South America

Map of Asia

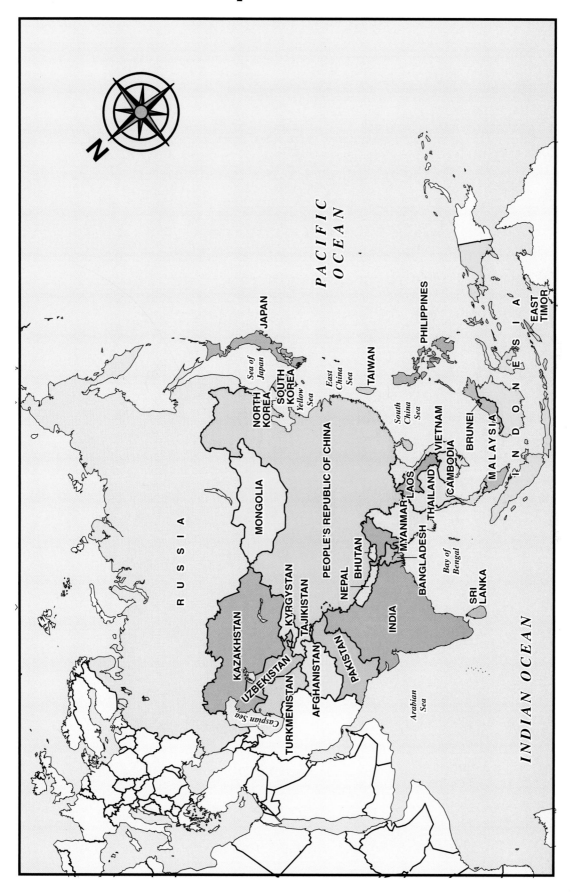

Map of the United States

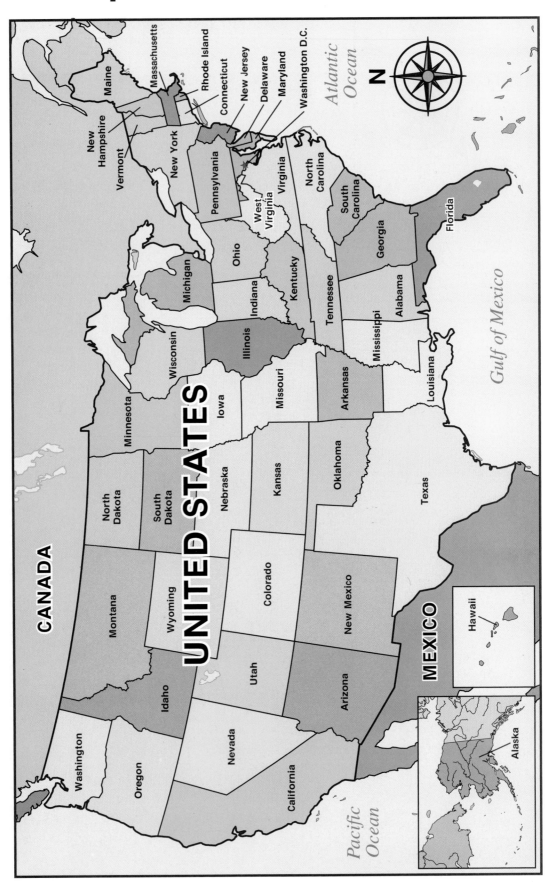